„Legen Sie los und erleben Sie das **neue Sprachenlernen**!"

Sprachkurs Englisch Bild für Bild
Herausgegeben von der Langenscheidt-Redaktion

Kreative Umsetzung: Arndt Knieper, Martin Waller
Texte: Stuart Amor, Dr. Helen Galloway, Dr. Lutz Walther
Art Direction, Layout, Zeichnungen: Arndt Knieper
Redaktion: Martin Waller, Werkstatt München – Buchproduktion
Projektleitung: Dorothea Leiser, Marc Strittmatter, Stefanie Templin
Corporate Design Umschlag: KW 43 BRANDDESIGN, Düsseldorf
Umschlaggestaltung: Guter Punkt, München
Fotos Innenteil: Bildnachweis als PDF auf der beiliegenden CD

Auf **www.langenscheidt.de/Sprachkurs-Bild-fuer-Bild** steht Ihnen das kostenlose Zusatzangebot Ihres Englisch-Sprachkurses zur Verfügung. Geben Sie dazu bitte den Code **ESB222** ein.

www.langenscheidt.de
© 2017 Langenscheidt GmbH & Co. KG, München
Satz: Anja Dengler, Werkstatt München
Druck und Bindung: Druckerei C. H. Beck, Nördlingen

ISBN: 978-3-468-27010-9

17010

Langenscheidt

Sprachkurs
Englisch
Bild für Bild

Der visuelle Kurs für den leichten Einstieg

von Stuart Amor

Langenscheidt

München · Wien

INHALT

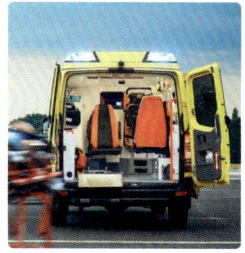

AUF DER CD _____

TONAUFNAHMEN (MP3):
Dialoge // Wortschatz //
Hörübungen

TEXTE (PDF):
Dialoge mit deutscher
Übersetzung // Hörtexte //
Bildnachweis

SO FUNKTIONIERT DIESER KURS

Jedes Kapitel besteht aus sechs Teilen

1

DIALOGWORTSCHATZ

Hier finden Sie alle Wörter, die im Dialog auf der Seite gegenüber neu eingeführt werden. Am leichtesten fällt Ihnen der Einstieg, wenn Sie sich zuerst mit den Vokabeln beschäftigen — aber Sie können auch gleich mit dem Dialog beginnen. In jedem Fall haben Sie das neue Wort und seine Bedeutung sofort im Blick.

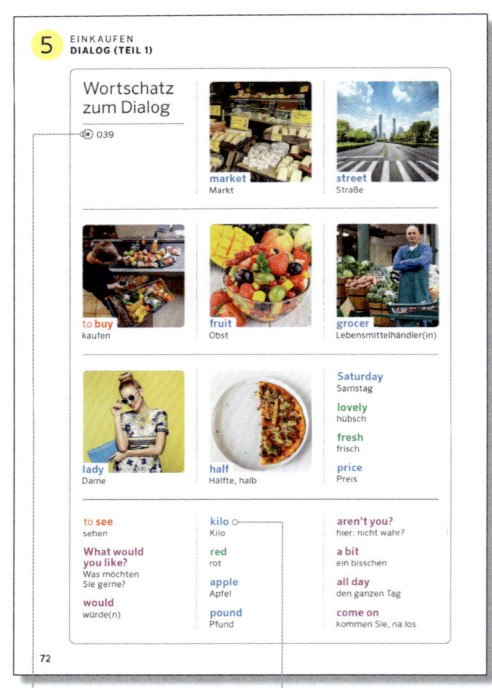

Der Farbcode

Sie wundern sich, warum die Texte so bunt sind? In diesem Kurs wird durchgängig ein Farbcode angewendet, der Ihnen bei allen neuen Vokabeln sofort die Wortart anzeigt. Auch auf den Grammatikseiten finden sich diese Farben wieder.

Es ist ganz einfach:

Substantive = blau

Verben = rot

Adjektive und Adverbien = grün

Funktionswörter und Redewendungen = violett

Wie die Wörter ausgesprochen werden, hören Sie auf der CD; die jeweilige Tracknummer steht hier.

Die Farbmarkierung zeigt nicht nur die Wortart an, sie hilft auch beim schnellen Auffinden der Vokabeln.

2

DIALOG IN ZWEI TEILEN

Die Dialoge erzählen eine unterhaltsame Geschichte: Die junge Stuttgarterin Paula ist eben nach London gekommen, freundet sich mit ihrem Kollegen Philip und dessen Familie an und unternimmt eine Dienstreise in die USA.

Da kleine Einheiten das Lernen erleichtern, sind die Dialoge zweigeteilt. Wie sie auf Englisch klingen, ist auf der CD zu hören.

3

THEMENWORTSCHATZ

Nach dem Dialog folgt ein zusätzlicher, individuell bebilderter Wortschatz, in dem einzelne Themenbereiche vertieft werden. Auch diese Vokabeln sind vollständig vertont.

Alle Dialoge werden professionell gesprochen, die der ersten Kapitel sogar zusätzlich nochmals in langsamerem Tempo.

Mit den Fragen zum Dialog können Sie testen, wie gut Sie schon alles verstanden haben.

4

WORTSCHATZ-ÜBUNGEN

Damit sich Ihnen die neu gelernten Vokabeln noch besser einprägen, folgt nun eine Seite mit Übungen, in denen Sie den neuen Wortschatz anwenden können.

*Alle Lösungen
finden Sie im Anhang
ab Seite 274*

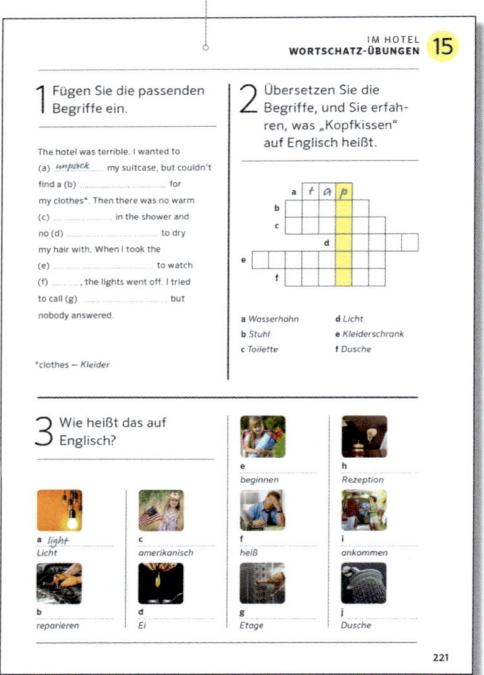

5

GRAMMATIK

So einfach lässt sich Grammatik erklären! Verbformen, Genitivbildung, Adverbien … alles, was dazugehört, um ganze Sätze zu bilden und sich richtig zu unterhalten, wird mit eigens dafür entwickelten Illustrationen verdeutlicht. Sie werden sehen, wie sich auf witzige Weise sofort ein Aha-Effekt einstellt.

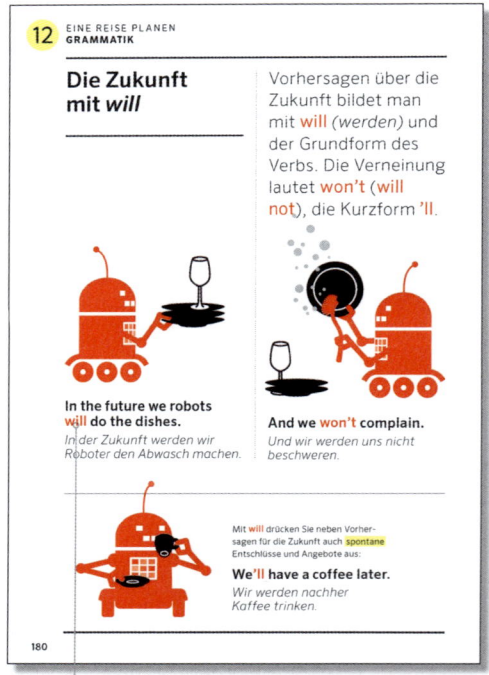

*Auch hier finden Sie
wieder den Farbcode,
den Sie schon vom
Dialogwortschatz her
kennen.*

6

GRAMMATIK-ÜBUNGEN

Ohne Fleiß kein Preis. Aber wahrscheinlich brennen Sie schon darauf, Ihr neues Wissen anzuwenden. Die Übungen am Ende jedes Kapitels sind dafür genau richtig.

Die kleinen Illustrationen verweisen auf das jeweilige Grammatik-Thema.

Manche Übungen trainieren speziell das Hören und Sprechen. Die dazugehörige Tracknummer auf der CD steht hier.

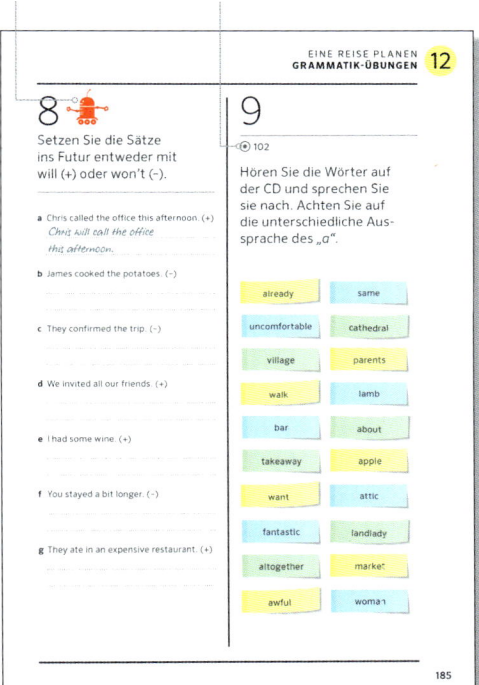

Zwischen- und Abschlusstests

Zwei Zwischentests und ein Abschlusstest ermöglichen es Ihnen, Ihren Lernfortschritt selbst zu überprüfen.

Anhang

Im Anhang finden Sie alles, was Sie außerdem noch für einen guten Lernerfolg brauchen: Die Lösungen zu allen Übungen und Testaufgaben, eine Verbtabelle, eine Übersicht der grammatischen Begriffe, eine Anleitung zur Aussprache sowie ein alphabetisches Gesamtverzeichnis der im Kurs verwendeten Vokabeln mit Angabe der Lautschrift.

Beiliegende CD

Um Sie auch beim Hören und Sprechen zu unterstützen, enthält die beigelegte CD Tonaufnahmen aller Dialoge, des gesamten Wortschatzes und der Übungen, bei denen Hörverständnis verlangt wird. Alles wurde von Muttersprachlern professionell eingesprochen.

Darüber hinaus finden Sie auf der CD ein Dokument im praktischen PDF-Format mit allen Dialogen inkl. deutscher Übersetzung sowie den Hörübungen zum Nachlesen.

Alle Inhalte der CD können Sie sich außerdem kostenlos auf unserer Website herunterladen (siehe Impressum).

Abkürzungen

Folgende Abkürzungen werden verwendet:

Sg — Singular   sth. — something
Pl — Plural   etw. — etwas

1 BEGRÜSSUNG

In diesem Kapitel lernen Sie

jemanden zu begrüßen →

nach dem Befinden zu fragen und darauf zu antworten →

jemanden vorzustellen →

Wortschatz zum Dialog

◎ 002

Weitere Vokabeln zu diesem Dialog finden Sie im Themenwortschatz auf Seite 16 und 17.

Welcome!
Willkommen!

morning
Morgen

to **talk**
sprechen

to **show**
zeigen

office
Büro

to
zu, nach; hier: in

good
gut

today
heute

fine
fein, prima

everything
alles

this
dies, das (hier)

from
aus, von

nice
hübsch, schön, nett

to **have (got)**
haben

with
mit; hier: bei

us
uns

where
wo

in
in

the
der/die/das

south
Süden

of
von

yes
ja

to **know**
kennen, wissen

but
aber

don't (know)
nicht (wissen)

can
können

and
und

to **meet**
(sich) treffen

too
auch

Welcome
to England!
in

◉ 003 & 004

 PHILIP: Good morning, John. How are you today?

 **JOHN:** Fine, thanks. Everything's OK.

 This is Paula Schneider. She's from Germany.
is

 PAULA: Good morning.

 Hello, Paula. Nice to have you with us. Where are you from in Germany?

 I'm from Stuttgart — in the south of Germany.
von

 Oh, yes. I know Munich, but I don't know Stuttgart.

 Paula can talk to the boss. And I can show Paula the offices.

 Hi, Hazel. Paula, this is Hazel.

 HAZEL: Hello, Paula. Nice to meet you.

 Nice to meet you, too.

— Paula is from
  ☐ England
  ☐ Germany.
— Paula is from
  ☐ Stuttgart
  ☐ Munich.

13

Marketing – niitxa – ausrichtung auf die Absatzförderung

◎ 006 & 007

JOHN: And this is Joyce Marlow, our Head of Marketing.

PAULA: Hello, Mrs Marlow.

JOYCE: You can just call me Joyce, Paula.

Mr Butler's got a problem with his new computer, Hazel. You're the expert.

HAZEL: OK, I can help him.

PHILIP: Come and meet Mr Butler. And then we can go round the offices.

OK, that's a good idea.

Oh, here's Mr Butler now. Good morning, Mr Butler. This is Paula Schneider from Germany.

MR BUTLER: Nice to meet you, Paula. Welcome to England!

— Joyce Marlow ☐ is ☐ isn't the boss.
— Mr Butler ☐ is ☐ isn't the Head of Marketing.

?

Wortschatz zum Dialog

◎ 005

Weitere Vokabeln zu diesem Dialog finden Sie im Themenwortschatz auf Seite 16 und 17.

head
Kopf; hier: Leiter(in)

to call
(an)rufen; hier: nennen

new
neu

to help
helfen

to come
kommen

to go
gehen, fahren

idea
Idee

here
hier

our unser(e)	**problem** Problem	**then** dann
just einfach, nur	**his** sein(e)	**round** herum
me mich, mir	**expert** Experte, Expertin	**that** das (dort), jenes
a/an ein(e)	**him** ihn, ihm	**now** nun, jetzt

Begrüßung und Verabschiedung

◉ 008

Where are you from?
Woher kommen Sie?

Good morning, Ms ...
Guten Morgen, Frau ...

My name is ...
Ich heiße ...

Nice to meet you, Mr ...
Schön, Sie kennenzulernen, Herr ...

How are you?
Wie geht's dir? /
Wie geht es Ihnen?

Fine, thanks.
Gut, danke.

Hello! Hi!
Hallo!

Goodbye!
Auf Wiedersehen!

Good afternoon!
Guten Tag!

Good evening!
Guten Abend!

See you soon.
Bis bald.

Bye bye.
Tschüs.

Personal-pronomen

◉ 009

I
ich

you
du, Sie

he
er

she
sie

it
es

we
wir

you
ihr, Sie

they
sie

1 Bringen Sie die beiden Dialoge in die passende Reihenfolge. Nummerieren Sie die Sätze jeweils von 1 bis 4.

a ..... OK, see you soon.

_1_ Hi, David, how are you?

..... Bye bye, Ms Holm.

..... Good morning, Ms Holm,
I'm fine, thanks.

b ..... Where are you from?

..... Hi, Ellen, nice to meet you.
My name is Henry.

..... Good afternoon, I'm Ellen.

..... I'm from Germany.

2 Ergänzen Sie die fehlenden Wörter.

| Nice | meet | you |
| name | Hello | thanks |

Hello! My (a) _name_ is Robert.

(b) .... Robert, I'm Mary.

Nice to (c) .... you.

(d) .... to meet you, too, Mary.

How are (e) .... today?

I'm fine, (f) ...., and you?

I'm fine, too. See you soon.

Bye bye.

3 Wie heißt das auf Englisch?

a _office_
Büro

b
Kopf

c
kommen

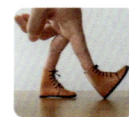

d
gehen

e
neu

f
Morgen

g
Willkommen!

h
sprechen

i
hier

j
wir

Das Verb *to be*

Die Formen des Verbs **to be** *(sein)* lauten in der einfachen Gegenwart:

Im gesprochenen Englisch werden viele Wörter verkürzt (siehe nächste Seite), insbesondere auch **to be**. Die Tabelle zeigt auch diese Kurzformen.

I'm an actor.
Ich bin Schauspieler.

LANGFORM	KURZFORM	
I **am**	I**'m**	*ich bin*
you **are**	you**'re**	*du bist / Sie sind (Sg)*
he/she/it **is**	he**'s**/she**'s**/it**'s**	*er/sie/es ist*
we **are**	we**'re**	*wir sind*
you **are**	you**'re**	*ihr seid / Sie sind (Pl)*
they **are**	they**'re**	*sie sind*

Verneint wird **to be** mit dem Zusatz **not**, in der Regel ebenfalls mit Kurzformen, die auf zwei Arten gebildet werden können (Ausnahme: 1. Person).

I**'m** not	—
you**'re** not	you **aren't**
he**'s** not / she**'s** not / it**'s** not	he **isn't** / she **isn't** / it **isn't**
we**'re** not	we **aren't**
you**'re** not	you **aren't**
they**'re** not	they **aren't**

I'm not an actor.
Ich bin kein Schauspieler.

Kurzformen

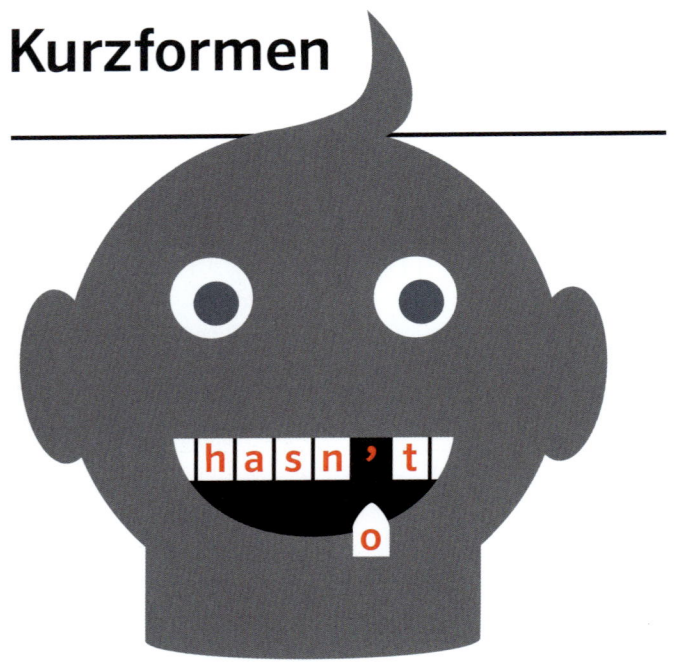

Häufig verwendete Kurzformen gibt es nicht nur für **to be**, sondern auch für **has/have** und für die Verneinung **not**.

LANGFORM	KURZFORM
am	'm
are	're
is	's
has	's
have	've
not	n't

He hasn't got all of his teeth anymore.
Er hat nicht mehr alle seine Zähne.

Beachten Sie, dass **'s** sowohl für **is** als auch für **has** stehen kann.

Die Artikel

I see a car.
Ich sehe ein Auto.

I see the car.
Ich sehe das Auto.

Der bestimmte Artikel lautet im Englischen **the** *(der/die/das)*. Er bleibt unverändert und kann vor allen Substantiven stehen, sowohl im Singular als auch im Plural.

Der unbestimmte Artikel **a** *(ein/eine)* wird vor Wörtern, die mit einem gesprochenen Vokal beginnen, zu **an** erweitert:
an office *ein Büro*,
an expert *ein Experte/ eine Expertin*.

4

Setzen Sie die richtigen Pronomen ein.

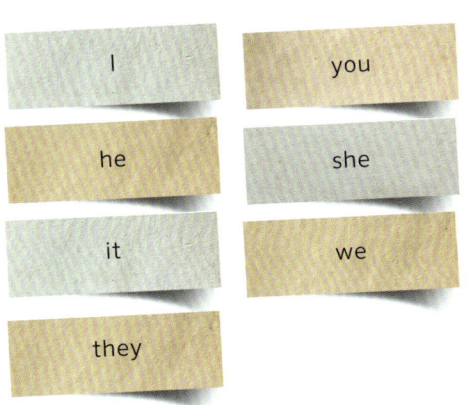

I

you

he

she

it

we

they

a How are *you* .... ?

.... 'm OK, thanks.

b Look, that's Paula. .... 's
from Stuttgart.

c This is Mr Butler's computer.

.... 's new.

d Mr Butler can help.

.... 's the boss.

e Where are Paula and the boss?

.... 're in his office.

f How are you and Joyce?

.... 're OK.

5

Ergänzen Sie nach dem Muster alle Kurzformen, die möglich sind.

a we are not   *we aren't*
                    we're not

b he is not

....

....

c you are not   ....

....

d I am not   ....

....

e she is not   ....

....

f they are not   ....

....

g it is not   ....

....

6

Lesen Sie die E-Mail und ersetzen Sie die Langformen durch Kurzformen.

To: k.evin@om-mail.com
Cc:
Subject: computers :(
From: j.hurt@ichi... Signature: None

Hi Kevin,

we are OK. I am fine and Hazel is OK, too. She is here! Jenny is not here, but she is fine. Hazel has got a computer, too. It is new. Computers! They are a problem, and I am not an expert. Oh, you are a computer expert — you can help!…

Kind regards*
John

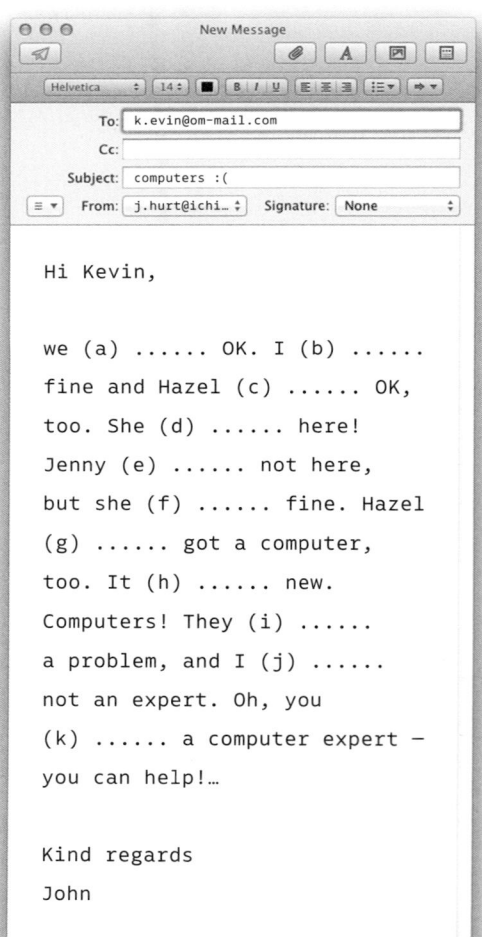

To: k.evin@om-mail.com
Cc:
Subject: computers :(
From: j.hurt@ichi... Signature: None

Hi Kevin,

we (a) ...... OK. I (b) ...... fine and Hazel (c) ...... OK, too. She (d) ...... here! Jenny (e) ...... not here, but she (f) ...... fine. Hazel (g) ...... got a computer, too. It (h) ...... new. Computers! They (i) ...... a problem, and I (j) ...... not an expert. Oh, you (k) ...... a computer expert — you can help!…

Kind regards
John

*Kind regards — *Liebe Grüße*

7

Verneinen Sie die Sätze.

a Paula Schneider is from England.
Paula Schneider isn't from England.

b She's from Munich.

c I'm the Head of Marketing.

d Mr Butler is a computer expert.

e We're OK this morning.

f They're in Mr Butler's office.

g Hazel, you're the Head of Marketing.

h This is Mr Butler's computer.

8

◎ 010

In der Kantine: Hören Sie die CD und reagieren Sie entsprechend den deutschen Vorgaben.

Welcome to England!

I know Stuttgart. It's nice.

Nice to meet you.

Nice to have you with us.

Where are you from?

Fine, thanks.

2
KENNENLERNEN UND SMALL TALK

In diesem Kapitel lernen Sie

jemandem etwas anzubieten →

von Ihrer Arbeit zu berichten →

über regelmäßige Handlungen zu reden →

Wortschatz zum Dialog

◉ 011

Weitere Vokabeln zu diesem Dialog finden Sie im Themenwortschatz auf Seite 30 und 31.

typical
typisch

coffee
Kaffee

milk
Milch

tea
Tee

people
Leute, Menschen

to drink
trinken

at home
zu Hause

sugar
Zucker

day	**why**	**to ask**
Tag	warum	fragen
please	**not**	**no**
bitte	nicht	nein; kein(e)
Here you are.	**always**	**for**
bitte schön	immer	für
thank you, thanks	**work**	
danke	Arbeit	

A **typical day**

◎ 012 & 013

 **PHILIP:** Coffee, Paula?

 PAULA: Yes, please.

 With milk?

 Please.

 Here you are.

 Thank you. But why have you got coffee? Why not tea? English people always drink tea!

 Not always. I drink tea at home and coffee at work. Don't ask me why! Where's the sugar?

 Here you are.

 Thanks. No sugar for you?

 No, thanks. Not for me.

— **Philip drinks**
  ☐ tea ☐ coffee at work.
— **Sugar for Paula?**
  ☐ yes ☐ no

◉ 015 & 016

PHILIP: What's your work like, Paula?

PAULA: Well, it's like your
work here. You know I work
for InterSoft in Stuttgart and
I plan new projects. I usually
work in a team. We have
meetings every week.

nie

Ah, those meetings! We have
them every day!

Sitzungen

We sometimes talk for hours
about one little thing!

I know! What's a typical day in
the life of Paula Schneider?

What can I say? I always do
the same things in the morning.
I always check my e-mails first
and answer them. It usually
takes me two or three hours,
but the phone often rings and
rings. Then it takes me longer.
I have lunch in our canteen.
After that I sometimes talk
to my colleagues or my boss.
Sometimes it's very boring!
And I never get home before six.

— Paula plans new
  ☐ meetings ☐ projects.
— Philip has meetings
  ☐ every week ☐ every day.
— Paula ☐ sometimes ☐ never
  gets home before six.

Wortschatz zum Dialog

◉ 014

Weitere Vokabeln zu diesem Dialog finden Sie im Themenwortschatz auf Seite 30 und 31.

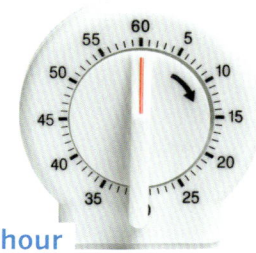

hour
Stunde

to say
sagen

the same
der-/die-/dasselbe

lunch
Mittagessen

What's ... like?
Wie ist ... ?

What's your work like?
Wie ist deine Arbeit?

well
nun, also

like
wie, als

usually normalerweise	**thing** Ding, Sache	**or** oder
every jede(r, s)	**life** Leben	**often** oft
week Woche	**what** was	**longer** länger
those diese, jene	**to do** tun, machen	**after** nach
them sie *(Pl)*	**my** mein(e)	**very** sehr
sometimes manchmal	**first** zuerst; erste(r, s)	**never** nie
about über, von	**to answer** (be)antworten	**to get home** nach Hause kommen
little klein	**to take** nehmen; hier: dauern, (Zeit) brauchen	**before** vor *(zeitlich)*

Im Büro

◎ 017

team
Team

work
Arbeit

to work
arbeiten

boss
Chef(in)

phone
Telefon

meeting
Sitzung

colleague
Kollege/Kollegin

to plan
planen

to check
überprüfen, kontrollieren
tschek

to ring
klingeln

boring
langweilig

canteen
Kantine, Cafeteria

staff
Personal

project
tschekt
Projekt

e-mail
E-Mail

Die Zahlen

◉ 018

 **one**
eins

 **two**
zwei

 **three**
drei

 **four**
vier

 **five**
fünf

 **six**
sechs

 **seven**
sieben

 **eight**
acht

 **nine**
neun

 **ten**
zehn

 **eleven**
elf

 **twelve**
zwölf

 **thirteen**
dreizehn

 **fourteen**
vierzehn

 **fifteen**
fünfzehn

 **sixteen**
sechzehn

 **seven-
teen**
siebzehn

 **eighteen**
achtzehn

 **nineteen**
neunzehn

 **twenty**
zwanzig

 **twenty-
one**
einund-
zwanzig

 **twenty-
two**
zweiund-
zwanzig

 **thirty**
dreißig

 **thirty-
one**
einund-
dreißig

 **forty**
vierzig

 **fifty**
fünfzig

 **sixty**
sechzig

 **seventy**
siebzig

 **eighty**
achtzig

 **ninety**
neunzig

 **a/one
hundred**
hundert

 **(one)
hundred
and one**
(ein)hundert-
undeins

 **zero**
null

*Die Ziffer 0
wird in
Telefon-
nummern
entweder
„oh" oder
„zero" ge-
sprochen.*

1 Welches Wort passt? Unterstreichen Sie das richtige Wort.

a Meetings are <u>boring</u> / bossing.

b I'm on the canteen / phone all day.

c We write coffees / e-mails and answer the phone.

d Sandy is a nice colleague / college.

e I work in a fax / team.

f My work / sugar starts at 8 in the morning.

g I ring / check my e-mails every morning.

2 Schreiben Sie die Zahlen aus.

a 2 _two_ ....

b 4 ....

c 7 ....

d 9 ....

e 11 ....

f 15 ....

g 22 ....

h 31 ....

i 40 ....

j 56 ....

3 Wie heißt das auf Englisch?

a _at home_
zu Hause

b
Mittagessen

c
Leute

d
trinken

e
Stunde

f
sagen

g
Zucker

h
Milch

i
typisch

j
dasselbe

Häufigkeitsadverbien

Adverbien der Häufigkeit stehen in der Regel <mark>direkt vor dem Verb</mark>.

It usually rains in Dublin.
In Dublin regnet es normalerweise.

Pengins always live in groups.
Pinguine leben immer in Gruppen.

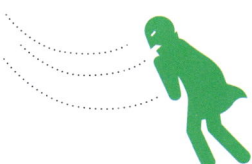

The wind often blows at the seaside.
An der Küste bläst oft der Wind.

It sometimes snows in April.
Manchmal schneit es im April.

It never rains in California.
In Kalifornien regnet es nie.

Der Plural von Substantiven

Den Plural von Substantiven bilden Sie in der Regel durch Anhängen von **-s**.

an apple
ein Apfel

two apples
zwei Äpfel

Possessivpronomen

my	*mein(e)*
your	*dein(e)/Ihr(e)*
his	*sein(e)*
her	*ihr(e)*
its	*sein(e)*
our	*unser(e)*
your	*euer(e)/Ihr(e)*
their	*ihr(e)*

This is my teddy.
Das ist mein Teddy.

The cat loves our new armchair.
Die Katze liebt unseren neuen Sessel.

Einfache Gegenwart

Die Verbformen der einfachen Gegenwart (*simple present*) entsprechen meist der Grundform. Nur bei der 3. Person Singular (**he/she/it**) wird in der Regel ein **-s** an das Verb angehängt.

z.B. to talk	
I **talk**	we **talk**
you **talk**	you **talk**
he/she/it **talks**	they **talk**

He sits on the floor.
Er sitzt auf dem Boden.

Merken Sie sich:
he/she/it – das **-s** muss mit!

4

Setzen Sie die richtigen Wörter ein.

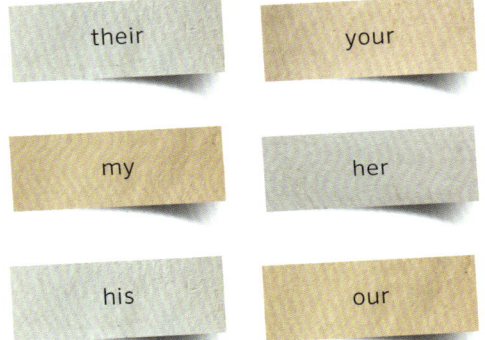

their · your · my · her · his · our

a Here you are. Here's
your coffee.

b We can have lunch in
.... canteen.

c I always check ....
e-mails first.

d That's my colleague. ....
name's John.

e She's in the team, too. ....
name's Hazel.

f John and Hazel have ....
coffee at ten.

5

Reagieren Sie auf diese Fragen und verwenden Sie dabei die Wörter *sometimes, always, often, usually* oder *never.*

a I usually drink coffee. And you?
I never drink coffee.

b Paula never drinks tea with milk. What
about you? / ....

c I always answer my e-mails. And you?
/ ....

d I never drink coffee at work. You?
/ ....

e Philip sometimes works at home. And
what about you?
/ ....

6

Finden Sie die passenden englischen Entsprechungen zu den deutschen Sätzen und sprechen Sie sie laut aus.

b
München kenne ich nicht.

2
Sometimes it's boring.

a
Engländer trinken immer Tee!

1
Welcome to England!

c
Manchmal ist es langweilig.

4
He's from Germany.

d
Er ist aus Deutschland.

3
English people always drink tea!

e
Willkommen in England!

5
I don't know Munich.

7

Lesen Sie den Tagesablauf
und ergänzen Sie die
passenden Verben (Mehr-
fachnennungen möglich).
Denken Sie daran:
he/she/it — das -s muss mit!

drink   get   talk

have   check

A typical day:

In the morning I (a) *drink* coffee
first and then I (b) .... my
e-mails.

My colleagues always (c) .... tea!
My boss (d) .... to me in the
morning.

We often (e) .... meetings, too.
I never (f) .... home before six,
but my boss never (g) .... home
before eight!

8

◉ 019

Kaffee oder Tee? Hören
Sie die CD und kreuzen Sie
die richtige Lösung an.

a ☐ Coffee, but no milk.
  ☐ Coffee with milk.

b ☐ Tea with sugar.
  ☐ Tea with milk.

c ☐ Coffee with sugar.
  ☐ Coffee with sugar and milk.

d ☐ Tea with sugar and milk.
  ☐ Tea, but no sugar and no milk.

9

Unterstreichen Sie die
passende Singular- oder
Pluralform.

a They haven't got an office/offices in
  London now.

b We have two meeting/meetings every
  week.

c Paula has two computer/computers
  in her office.

d She's in London for a week/weeks.

e Philip answers five e-mail/e-mails.

f The meeting takes an hour/hours.

3

ÜBER SICH
SELBST SPRECHEN

In diesem Kapitel lernen Sie

Fragen zu stellen und zu beantworten →

Gefühle zu äußern →

über sich selbst zu sprechen →

Wortschatz zum Dialog

◎ 020

happy
glücklich

surprised
überrascht
ʊ praɪsd

old
alt

dead
tot

school
Schule

to **look at**
ansehen

to **look**
schauen;
hier: aussehen

friend
Freund(in)

awful
schrecklich

year
Jahr

wife
Ehefrau

to **live**
leben; wohnen

son
Sohn

mum
Mama

to **like**
mögen, gern haben

to **feel**
(sich) fühlen

lonely
einsam

to **want**
wollen

to **surf**
surfen

to **chat**
chatten; plaudern

on
an, auf; hier: im

dad
Papa

time
Zeit

interest
Interesse

to **go out**
ausgehen,
weggehen

hardly ever
fast nie

to **phone**
anrufen

Problems, problems!

◎ 021 & 022

PHILIP: Just look at you! You don't look very happy, my friend. I'm not surprised. Look at your life. Awful! You're forty-three years old. Your wife is dead. You live here with your son and your mum. Andy doesn't like school. Mum says she feels lonely and wants to meet people. She's got her new computer now and she wants to surf and chat on the Internet.

ANDY: Dad!

And do you have time for your interests? No — it's just work, work, work. Have you got time? No, you haven't. Can you go out? No, you can't. You hardly ever meet friends, and they don't ever phone you …

— Philip ☐ looks happy
☐ doesn't look happy.
— Philip's mother has got
☐ a new computer
☐ a new phone.

◉ 024 & 025

 **ANDY:** Dad! Dad! Phone for you. Sounds foreign! Are you upstairs?

 PHILIP: Yes, I am. Coming! ... Hello?

 PAULA: Hello, Philip. It's Paula here.

 Hi, Paula. How are you?

 Well, not too good, to be honest.

 Really? What's wrong?

 I don't know. Everything. I can't understand my landlady here in this B&B — she's from Scotland. I feel uncomfortable here in this little room. The landlady's cooking is terrible. Baked beans with every meal. I can't find a flat. They're all too expensive. And I don't know anyone. I just feel depressed.

 Paula, I've got an idea. Have you got time to go out this evening?

 Yes, I have. That's a great idea.

— Paula understands her landlady.
☐ right ☐ wrong
— The landlady is from
☐ Scotland ☐ Germany.

Wortschatz zum Dialog

◉ 023

upstairs
oben (im Haus)

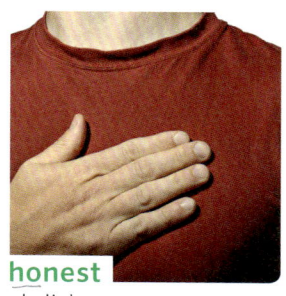

honest
ehrlich

uncomfortable
unbequem; hier: unwohl

expensive
teuer

evening
Abend

to **sound**
klingen

foreign
ausländisch

Coming!
(Ich) komme (schon)!

too
zu (sehr), allzu

really
wirklich

What's wrong?
Was ist los?

to **understand**
verstehen

landlady
Vermieterin

B&B (Bed and Breakfast)
Frühstücks-pension

Scotland
Schottland

room
Zimmer, Raum

cooking
Essen; Kochen

terrible
fürchterlich

baked beans
gebackene Bohnen
(in Tomatensauce)

meal
Mahlzeit

to **find**
finden

flat
Wohnung

all
alle; alles

anyone
(irgend)jemand

depressed
deprimiert

great
großartig

right
richtig

wrong
falsch

Familienmitglieder

◎ 026

father
Vater

mother
Mutter

grandmother
Großmutter

grandfather
Großvater

parents
Eltern

aunt
Tante

uncle
Onkel

cousin
Cousine

cousin
Cousin

daughter
Tochter

sister
Schwester

son
Sohn

brother
Bruder

siblings
Geschwister

wife
Ehefrau

husband
Ehemann

niece
Nichte

nephew
Neffe

single
unver-
heiratet,
ledig

**sepa-
rated**
getrennt

widowed
verwitwet

married
verheiratet

divorced
geschieden

1 Bezeichnen Sie das jeweilige „Gegenstück" in der Familie.

a brother *sister*

b husband

c grandmother

d uncle

e son

f niece

g mother

2 Welche Definition passt zu welchem Begriff?

1 when you're not married anymore*

2 when you no longer live with your partner

3 when you're not married

4 when you have a husband or a wife

5 when your husband or wife is dead

a married

b divorced

c single

d widowed

e separated

*not … anymore — nicht mehr

3 Wie heißt das auf Englisch?

a *honest*
ehrlich

b
glücklich

c
Schule

d
oben (im Haus)

e
tot

f
alt

g
Abend

h
unbequem

i
überrascht

j
teuer

45

Kurzantworten mit *be, can, have*

Im Englischen beant-wortet man Fragen oft mit Kurzantworten.

Bei **to be** *(sein)*, **to have** *(haben)* und **can** *(können)* wird das Verb in der Kurzantwort wiederholt. Ein einfaches „yes" oder „no" wirkt hingegen sehr abrupt.

Is he depressed?
Ist er bedrückt?

No, he **isn't**.
Nein.

Yes, he **is**.
Ja.

Have you got eggs?
Haben Sie Eier?

No, I **haven't**.
Nein.

Yes, I **have**.
Ja.

Can we go out?
Können wir ausgehen?

No, we **can't**.
Nein.

Yes, we **can**.
Ja.

Der s-Genitiv

Der Genitiv zeigt den ==Besitz== oder die ==Zu-gehörigkeit== an. Sie bil-den ihn bei Personen durch Anhängen von **s** mit Apostroph: **'s**.

Mary**'s** genitiv
lamb
Marys Lamm

Verneinung, Frage und Kurzantwort mit dem Hilfsverb *to do*

Sie können bereits bejahte Aussagen bilden. Für Verneinungen, Fragen (S. 48) und Kurzantworten (S. 48) brauchen Sie in der Regel das Hilfsverb to do (*tun, machen*). Auch hier weicht die 3. Person Singular von der Grundform ab. Sie lautet does.

I don't
like the soup.
*Ich mag die
Suppe nicht.*

Für eine Verneinung steht in der Regel **do not** direkt vor dem Vollverb (in der 3. Person **does not**), meist in der Kurzform don't/doesn't.

Thomas likes sausages.
Thomas mag Wurst.

He doesn't like vegetables.
Er mag kein Gemüse.

Auch für <mark>Fragen</mark> brauchen Sie das Hilfsverb **do/does**. Es steht dann vor dem Subjekt.

Magst du den Umzug?

Bei <mark>Kurzantworten</mark> rückt **do/does** nach hinten.

Ja, ich mag ihn.

Nein, ich mag ihn nicht.

Do they look happy?   **Yes, they do**.   **No, they don't**.
Sehen sie glücklich aus?   *Ja.*   *Nein.*

4

Beantworten Sie die Fragen mit Kurzantworten.

a Have you got time? Yes, *I have.*

b Can you go out? No, ...

c Has she got a computer? Yes, ...

....

d Has he got problems at work?

Yes, ...

e Are they at home? No, ...

f Are you in your room? Yes, ...

g Am I happy? No, ...

h Is he a computer expert? No, ...

....

5

Stellen Sie Fragen und geben Sie Kurzantworten mit *do* oder *does*.

a *Does* .... Andy like school?

No, he *doesn't.*

b .... Philip have time for his

interests? No, he ....

c .... Paula feel depressed?

Yes, she ....

d .... you have time for your

friends? .... , I ....

6

Genitiv oder Plural? Ergänzen Sie *'s* oder *-s*.

My (a) son *'s* .... new computer is

terrible. I work with (b) computer...........

but I'm not an expert.

I can't help him. My (c) colleague...........

friend works for InterSoft and he has got

five (d) computer........... at home.

He can help. I can only help with my

(e) mum .... old computer,

but not with the new (f) computer........... !

7

◉ 027

Hören Sie die Wörter auf der CD und sprechen Sie sie nach. Achten Sie auf die unterschiedliche Aussprache des „o".

colleague

longer

uncomfortable

come

room

welcome

mobile

wrong

how

know

hour

lonely

honest

those

too

good

project

cooking

sometimes

foreign

close

8

Lesen Sie den Text und ergänzen Sie 's oder -s.

a Philip.'.s......... life is awful.

b He............ 43 year............ old.

c He live............ with his son and mum.

d His mum feel............ lonely and she want............ to meet people.

e She............ got a new computer.

f She want............ to surf and chat.

g Philip has no time for his interest............ .

h It............ just work, work, work.

i He hardly ever meet............ friends.

j It............ Paula on the phone.

k She............ depressed.

l Everything............ wrong.

m Her landlady............ cooking is terrible.

n The flat............ are all too expensive.

o But Philip............ got a great idea!

9

Füllen Sie das Kreuzwort-rätsel aus. Wie lautet das Lösungswort?

a Tea or ...?
b English ... drink tea!
c Paula ... gets home after six.
d ... to England!
e We have a ... every day.
f Stuttgart and Munich are in ...
g Paula Schneider is in ...
h An ... is 60 minutes.
i Can you ... this question?

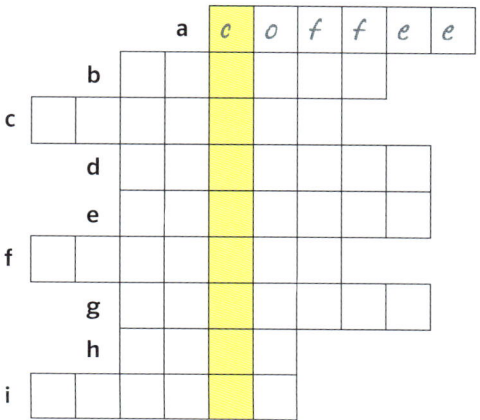

10

Verneinen Sie die folgenden positiven Sätze, indem Sie entweder *don't* oder *doesn't* vor dem Verb einfügen.

a I drink coffee every morning. *I don't drink coffee every morning.*

b We like our B&B in London.

c She always says thank you.

d You look happy today.

e They have time this evening.

f Philip finds his computer.

g Mum wants to meet people.

4
KULTURELLE UNTERSCHIEDE

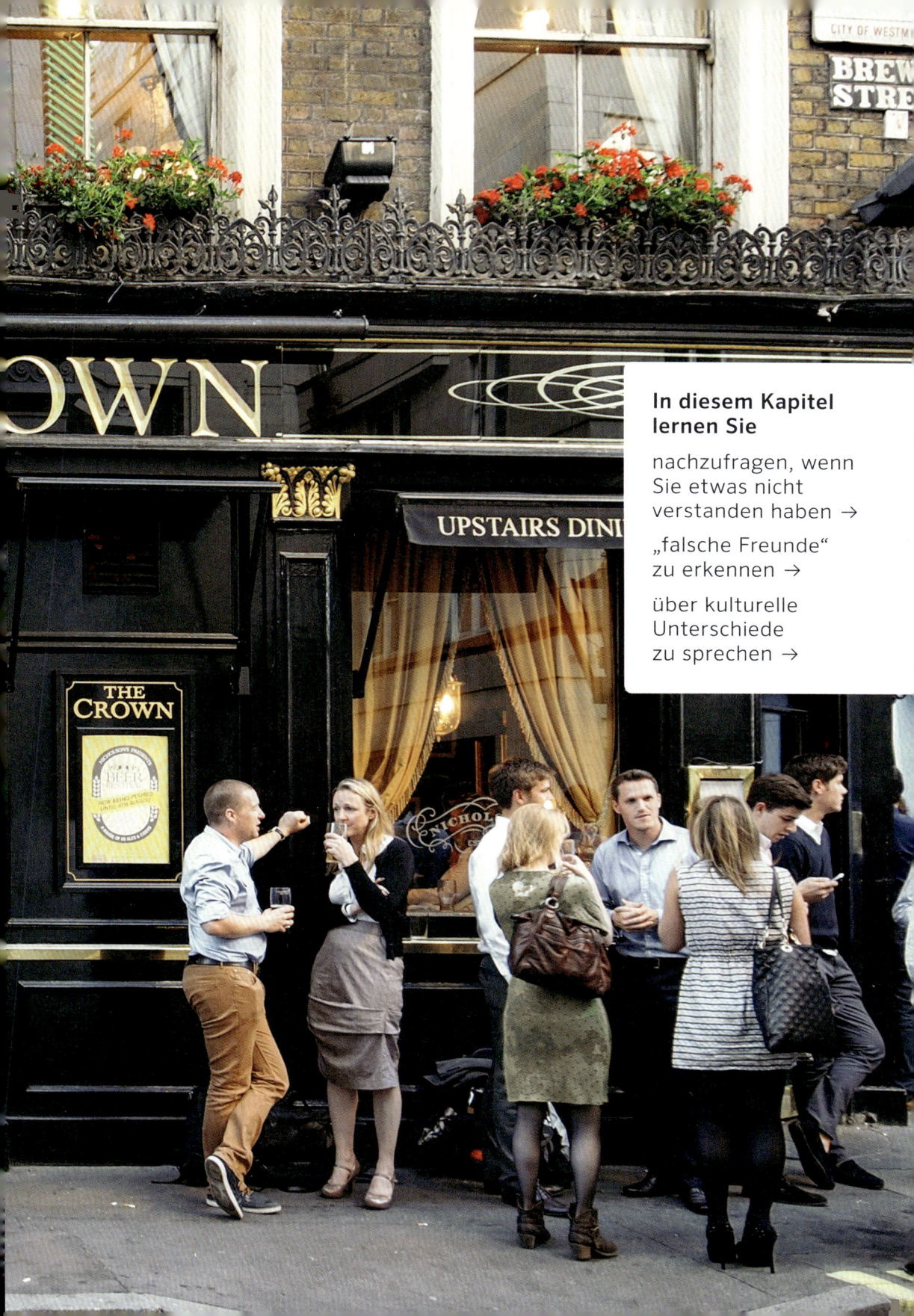

**In diesem Kapitel
lernen Sie**

nachzufragen, wenn
Sie etwas nicht
verstanden haben →

„falsche Freunde"
zu erkennen →

über kulturelle
Unterschiede
zu sprechen →

Wortschatz zum Dialog

◉ 028

Weitere Vokabeln zu diesem Dialog finden Sie im Themenwortschatz auf Seite 58 und 59.

pub
Pub, Kneipe

drink
Getränk

waiter
Kellner

bar
Theke

to pay
bezahlen

different
anders

I'd like (I would like)
ich möchte gerne

pint
Pint *(ca. ½ l)*

at
in, an, um

to get
bekommen, hier: holen

when
wann; wenn, als

each time
jedes Mal

to leave
verlassen

What about you?
Was ist mit dir?

like that
so, auf diese Weise

just a minute
einen Augenblick

minute
Minute

At the pub

◉ 029 & 030

PHILIP: Drink, Paula?

PAULA: Oh. Yes, please. Where's the waiter?

Waiter? There isn't a waiter in a pub. We go and get our drinks at the bar.

And when do you pay?

We pay when we get the drinks — at the bar. Each time, for the first, second, third drink …

Oh. It's different in Germany. We pay before we leave.

Really? Well, I'd like a pint. What about you?

I'd like a gin tonic, please.

A gin and tonic, we say.

But gin tonic is English!

Yes, but we don't say it like that. Just a minute (…) Here you are, Paula, your G and T.

— There ☐ is ☐ isn't
a waiter in the pub.
— In English pubs you pay
☐ at the bar ☐ when you leave.

◎ 032 & 033

 PAULA: That's my handy.

 PHILIP: What? What does that mean?

 Don't you say that in English?

 Oh, now I understand you. It's your mobile! That's English!

 English is so difficult! When English words aren't real English … And there are some English words like German words but they don't mean the same: Chef is a boss in German, and a cook in English.

 Hmm. And beer?

 Ah, that's nearly the same: Bier.

 One last drink, Paula! The pub closes at twelve o'clock.

 Good idea! Cheers!

— Chef means
  ☐ cook ☐ boss in English.
— The pub closes at
  ☐ eleven ☐ twelve o'clock.

Wortschatz zum Dialog

◎ 031

Weitere Vokabeln zu diesem Dialog finden Sie im Themenwortschatz auf Seite 58 und 59.

mobile (phone)
Handy, Mobiltelefon
mobail foun

difficult
schwierig, schwer

real
echt, wirklich

cook
Koch

beer
Bier

last
letzte(r, s)

to close
schließen

Cheers!
Prost! Zum Wohl!

to mean
bedeuten, meinen

in English
auf Englisch

so
so

word
Wort

there is/are
es gibt

some
einige; etwas

German
deutsch

chef
(Chef)Koch

nearly
fast

(12) o'clock
(12) Uhr

Ordnungs-zahlen von 1 bis 31

◎ 034

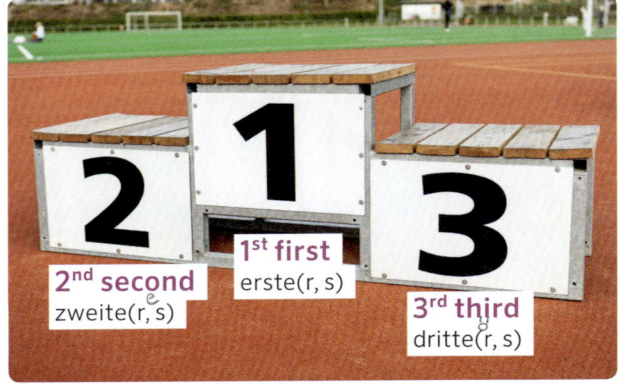

2nd second
zweite(r, s)

1st first
erste(r, s)

3rd third
dritte(r, s)

4th fourth
vierte(r, s)

5th fifth
fünfte(r, s)

6th sixth
sechste(r, s)

7th seventh
siebte(r, s)

8th eighth
achte(r, s)

9th ninth
neunte(r, s)

10th tenth
zehnte(r, s)

11th eleventh
elfte(r, s)

12th twelfth
zwölfte(r, s)

13th thirteenth
dreizehnte(r, s)

14th fourteenth
vierzehnte(r, s)

15th fifteenth
fünfzehnte(r, s)

20th twentieth
zwanzigste(r, s)

21st twenty-first
einundzwanzigste(r, s)

19th nineteenth
neunzehnte(r, s)

17th seventeenth
siebzehnte(r, s)

30th thirtieth
dreißigste(r, s)

16th sixteenth
sechzehnte(r, s)

18th eighteenth
achtzehnte(r, s)

31st thirty-first
einunddreißigste(r, s)

Falsche Freunde

Vorsicht bei Wörtern, die wie ein deutsches Wort klingen, im Englischen aber etwas ganz anderes bedeuten.

◉ 035

photograph
Foto

photographer
Fotograf(in)

gift
Geschenk

poison
Gift

sensible
vernünftig

sensitive
sensibel

to become
werden

to get
bekommen

brave
tapfer

well-behaved
brav

fabric
Stoff

plant, factory
Fabrik

1 Tragen Sie die richtige Ordnungszahl ein.

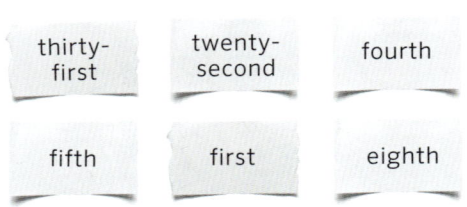

thirty-first | twenty-second | fourth

fifth | first | eighth

a Today is the *thirty-first* (31st) of May.

b I'm the .... (5th) child* in my family.

c The .... (4th) photograph is the best**.

d This is my .... (1st) beer today.

e The meeting is on the

.... (22nd).

f It's the .... (8th) book from the right.

* child – *Kind*; **best – *beste*

2 Welche Übersetzung ist richtig? Kreuzen Sie an.

a Fotograf
☐ photograph
☐ photographer

b Stoff
☐ fabric
☐ staff

c Gift
☐ gift
☐ poison

d bekommen
☐ to get
☐ to become

e vernünftig
☐ sensible
☐ sensitive

f Fabrik
☐ fabric
☐ plant

g Geschenk
☐ poison
☐ gift

h Foto
☐ photographer
☐ photograph

i brav
☐ brave
☐ well-behaved

3 Wie heißt das auf Englisch?

a *different*
anders

b
Koch

c
schließen

d
bezahlen

e
Kellner

f
schwierig

g
Handy

h
letzte(r, s)

i
Getränk

j
echt

Die Wiedergabe von „es gibt"

Wenn Sie sagen wollen, was es gibt und was es nicht gibt, verwenden Sie im Englischen im Singular **there is** und im Plural **there are**.

There are ghosts in the castle.

Es gibt Geister im Schloss.

Das gilt für Aussage, Frage, Kurzantwort und Verneinung.

There's a ghost!

There are ghosts!

Is there a ghost?

Are there ghosts?

Yes, there is!

Yes, there are!

There isn't a ghost.

There aren't ghosts.

Die Uhrzeit

Bei der Angabe von vollen Stunden werden rund um die Uhr die Zahlen von 1—12 verwendet.

Um zu verdeutlichen, ob sich die Uhrzeit auf den Vormittag oder den Nachmittag/Abend bezieht, ergänzen Sie die Zeitangabe, z.B. mit **in the morning** *morgens* oder **in the evening** *abends* oder durch das Kürzel **am** (vormittags) bzw. **pm** (nachmittags).

It's 6 o'clock in the morning.
It's 6 am.

Es ist sechs Uhr morgens.

It's 6 o'clock in the evening.
It's 6 pm.

Es ist sechs Uhr abends.

am pm

It's 12 o'clock.
Es ist 12 Uhr (mittags).

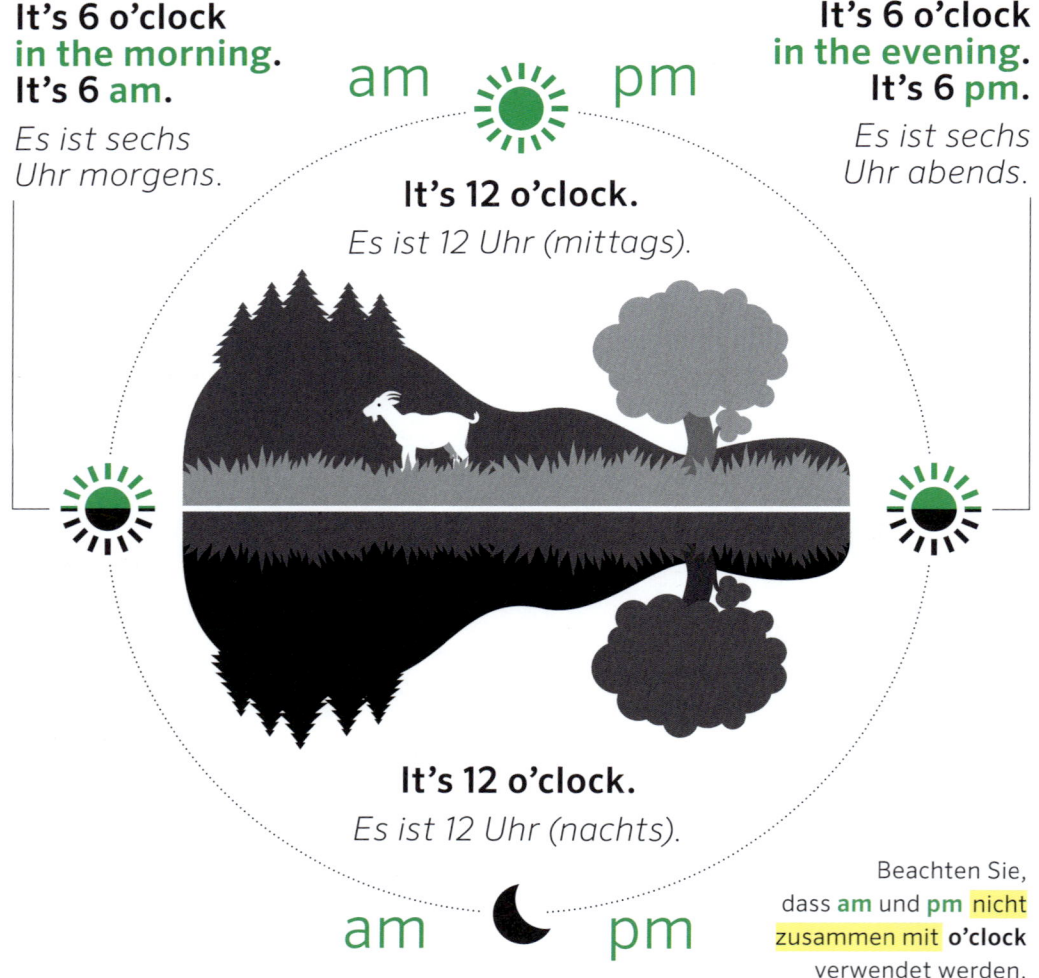

It's 12 o'clock.
Es ist 12 Uhr (nachts).

am pm

Beachten Sie, dass **am** und **pm** nicht zusammen mit **o'clock** verwendet werden.

4

Ergänzen Sie *there is*
oder *there are*.

a *There is* .... milk in this tea.

b .... problems with
the new computer.

c .... meetings every
week.

d .... no sugar in
this coffee.

e .... baked beans
with every meal.

f .... some nice flats
but they're expensive.

5

◉ 036

Vormittag oder
Nachmittag? Hören Sie
und kreuzen Sie an.

1 ☐ 3 am   **4** ☐ 5 am
   ☐ 3 pm   ☐ 5 pm

2 ☐ 11 am   **5** ☐ 9 am
   ☐ 11 pm   ☐ 9 pm

3 ☐ 8 am   **6** ☐ 2 am
   ☐ 8 pm   ☐ 2 pm

6

Welches Wort steht wo auf
der Liste? Lesen Sie die
Antworten laut vor.

coffee, tea, sugar,
baked beans, milk, bacon,
marmalade, crisps

a Coffee is *first* .... on the list.

b Baked beans are .... on the list.

c Crisps* are .... on the list.

d Tea is .... on the list.

e Marmalade is .... on the list.

f Bacon is .... on the list.

g Sugar is .... on the list.

h Milk is .... on the list.

* crisps — *Chips*

7

Nicht alle Wörter, die sich im Englischen und Deutschen ähneln, sind falsche Freunde. Die unterstrichenen Begriffe können Sie auch ohne Wörterbuch übersetzen!

Hi! My name's Tina. I'm 24 and I'm a (a) secretary in an (b) electronics firm. In my (c) free time I do (d) sports: (e) tennis, (f) basketball, and — yes — (g) football! I like (h) dancing at the (i) disco, and (j) shopping. I love (k) music, too, and I can play the (l) guitar. Please answer ...

a *Sekretärin*

b ....

c ....

d ....

e ....

f ....

g ....

h ....

i ....

j ....

k ....

l ....

8

Beantworten Sie die Fragen.

a Is there a waiter in an English pub?
   No, there isn't a waiter.
   ....

b Where do you get your drinks in a pub?
   ....
   ....

c When do you pay?
   ....
   ....

d When do you pay in Germany?
   ....
   ....

e What does Paula like to drink?
   ....
   ....

f What does the German word Handy mean?
   ....
   ....

g What does the English word chef mean?
   ....
   ....

h When does the pub close?
   ....
   ....

9

Small Talk: Finden Sie die passenden Antworten zu den Fragen?

1 Where's the sugar?

2 Coffee or tea?

3 Phone for you.

4 How are you?

5 Have you got time to go out?

6 Here's your drink.

7 I'd like a pint. What about you?

8 One last drink.

a Yes, good idea. Cheers!

b Well, not too good really.

c Thank you very much.

d A gin and tonic, please.

e Coming.

f Coffee for me, please.

g Here you are.

h Yes, that's a great idea.

Zwischentest 1

1 Was sagen Sie, wenn Sie ...

a ... jemanden zum ersten Mal treffen bzw. jemandem vorgestellt werden?

....

....

b ... jemanden in England willkommen heißen wollen?

....

....

c ... fragen wollen, was los/nicht in Ordnung ist?

....

....

d ... jemanden fragen möchten, ob er/sie Zeit hat, heute Abend auszugehen?

....

....

e ... sich sehr bedanken möchten?

....

....

f ... sagen möchten, dass etwas eine großartige Idee ist?

....

....

g ... fragen wollen, was ein bestimmtes Wort bedeutet?

....

....

○ **von 7 Punkten**

66

2 Welche Form des Verbs *to be* ist richtig? Kreuzen Sie an.

a ☐ Am
☐ Are
☐ Is
you OK today, Paula?

b Paula
☐ am
☐ are
☐ is
now in England.

c Joyce and Hazel
☐ am
☐ are
☐ is
in Mr Butler's office.

d Hazel
☐ am
☐ are
☐ is
a computer expert.

e I
☐ am
☐ are
☐ is
the Head of Marketing.

f We
☐ am
☐ are
☐ is
in the south of Germany.

◯ **von 6 Punkten**

3 Hören Sie drei Kurzporträts über Paula und Philip. Kreuzen Sie die richtigen Aussagen an.

◉ 037

a Paula is from
☐ Stuttgart.
☐ Munich.

b She has lunch
☐ at home.
☐ in their canteen.

c Philip Elton works for
☐ InterSoft.
☐ InterChip UK.

d He doesn't have time
☐ for his interests.
☐ for his work.

e Paula isn't happy because
☐ she hasn't got a room.
☐ everything is wrong.

f She can't find a flat because
☐ they are expensive.
☐ they are uncomfortable.

◯ **von 6 Punkten**

4 Welches Fragewort ist richtig? Kreuzen Sie es an.

a ☐ What ☐ How ☐ Why are you today?
b ☐ Where ☐ Why ☐ What are you from?
c ☐ Why ☐ How ☐ Where have you got coffee?
d ☐ How ☐ Where ☐ Why 's the sugar?
e ☐ Why ☐ What ☐ How 's wrong?
f ☐ Where ☐ Why ☐ What about you?

◯ **von 6 Punkten**

67

5 Lesen Sie die Visiten-karten und kreuzen Sie die richtigen Antworten an.

PAULA SCHNEIDER
InterSoft GmbH
Motorenstraße 10
D-70197 Stuttgart
Tel. 0711/47 89 23
.chneider@isoft.de

Philip Elton
InterChip UK
7 London Road
Islington EC1X 6BD
📞 020.7643 8122
n.elton@ichip.uk

JOYCE MARLOW
14 Camden Road
Islington EC1D 3SE
ph 020.6822 7693
joyce.marlow@web.uk

a Paula works in
☐ Munich.
☐ Stuttgart.

b InterChip UK is in
☐ London Road.
☐ Camden Road.

c Joyce Marlow lives in
☐ Camden.
☐ Islington.

6 Hören Sie die drei Kurz-dialoge und notieren Sie die Telefonnummern.

◉ 038

1 ....

2 ....

3 ....

⬤ **von 3 Punkten**

7 Welche Form ist richtig: *do* oder *does?* Kreuzen Sie an.

a ☐ Do ☐ Does
Paula feel depressed?

b ☐ Do ☐ Does
Paula know anyone?

c ☐ Do ☐ Does
she feel uncomfortable in her little room?

d ☐ Do ☐ Does
you feel happy?

e ☐ Do ☐ Does
Philip want to help?

f ☐ Do ☐ Does
your colleagues ever phone you?

8 Verneinen oder bejahen Sie die Sätze.

a Philip looks very happy.

....

b Andy likes school.

....

c Philip's mum doesn't feel lonely.

....

d She doesn't want to meet people.

....

e Paula feels fine in her little room.

....

f She doesn't feel depressed.

....

○ **von 6 Punkten**

9 Beantworten Sie die Fragen mit einer Kurzantwort.

a Are you at home? Yes, ...

b Can Paula understand her landlady? No, ...

c Does Paula feel uncomfortable in her room? Yes, ...

d Is the landlady's cooking terrible? Yes, ...

e Can Paula find a flat? No, ...

f Has she got time to go out? Yes, ...

○ **von 6 Punkten**

Sie haben

Punkte von 49 erreicht.

BEWERTUNG

45–49
★★★★
Very good
Kompliment! Ihre Mühe hat sich wirklich gelohnt.

35–44
★★★ **Good**
Prima — Sie haben sehr viel gelernt!

25–34
★★ OK
Vieles klappt schon ziemlich gut, aber üben Sie weiter an den Stellen, die Ihnen noch Schwierigkeiten bereiten.

Weniger als 25
★ **You can do better**
Sie können es noch besser. Die erste Etappe ist geschafft, aber es lohnt sich bestimmt, jetzt nochmals die Kapitel zu wiederholen, die Sie noch nicht so gut können.

5
EINKAUFEN

**In diesem Kapitel
lernen Sie**

höfliche Einkaufs-
gespräche zu
führen →

sich nach Waren
zu erkundigen →

das Datum
anzugeben →

Wortschatz zum Dialog

◎ 039

market
Markt

street
Straße

to buy
kaufen

fruit
Obst
frout

grocer
Lebensmittelhändler(in)

lady
Dame

half
Hälfte, halb

Saturday
Samstag

lovely
hübsch

fresh
frisch

price
Preis

to see
sehen

What would you like?
Was möchten Sie gerne?

would
würde(n)

kilo
Kilo

red
rot

apple
Apfel

pound
Pfund

aren't you?
hier: nicht wahr?

a bit
ein bisschen

all day
den ganzen Tag

come on
kommen Sie, na los

At the **market**

◎ 040 & 041

Paula has got a room in Islington. It is Saturday today and Paula goes to Chapel Market, one of the street markets in Islington. She wants to buy some fruit.

GROCER: Lovely fresh fruit! Lovely prices, too, my lovely lady!

PAULA: I'm not your lovely lady! I just want some fruit.

Well, you can see we've got lovely fresh fruit. What would you like?

Half a kilo of those red apples.

A pound of apples. You're new in London, aren't you? Things are a bit different here. Where are you from?

I'm from Stuttgart in Germany.

Welcome to England! And welcome to Chapel Market! Well, no time to chat all day. It's Saturday. Come on, ladies.

— **Chapel Market is in Islington.**
  ☐ right ☐ wrong
— **Paula wants** ☐ some fruit ☐ tea.

⊚ 043 & 044

 PAULA: Oh, sorry, could I have two of those lovely oranges, please?

 GROCER: Yes, of course. That's £ 3.45.

 Have you got any coffee?

 Yes, Italian coffee. It's very good.

 Hmmm. The sell-by date is 1st June. Is it still good?

 Yes, it's fine. The best-before date is 30th September. Would you like some?

 Yes, please. How much is it?

 It's £ 6.50. That's £ 9.95 altogether.

 Here's ten pounds.

 And five pence for you. Thank you.

— **The sell-by date of the coffee is 1st June.**
  ☐ right ☐ wrong
— **The grocer sells**
  ☐ German beer
  ☐ Italian coffee.

Wortschatz zum Dialog

◎ 042

sorry!
Entschuldigung!

any
etwas, irgendwelche(n)
e

Italian
italienisch

Italian
Italiener(in)

date
Datum
deit

best-before date
Haltbarkeitsdatum

much
viel
ol

altogether
(alles) zusammen
o

penny *(Pl pence)*
Penny *(engl. Währung, 100 p = £ 1)*

cud
could
könnte(n)

e
orange
Orange, Apfelsine

of course
natürlich

sell-by date
Verkaufsdatum

tschun
June
Juni

still
noch

ol
how
wie

Die Monate

◉ 045

Es gibt mehrere Möglichkeiten, das Datum anzugeben:
Sie schreiben **15th May** — *Sie sagen* **the fifteenth of May**
Sie schreiben **May 15th** — *Sie sagen* **May the fifteenth**
Sie schreiben **15 May/May 15** — *Sie sagen* **May fifteenth**

January
Januar

February
Februar

March
März

April
April
di

May
Mai
e

June
Juni
tschun

July
Juli
di

August
August
Ogast

September
September

October
Oktober

November
November

December
Dezember
is

1 Ergänzen Sie die fehlenden Wörter.

fresh	pound	pays
grocer	street	buy

Chapel Market is one of the (a) *street* markets in Islington.

There is a (b) .... who sells

(c) .... fruit.

Paula asks for a (d) .... of apples.

She wants to (e) .... some coffee, too, and (f) .... £ 9.95 altogether.

2 Gehen Sie einkaufen. Auf der Liste steht, was Sie brauchen und wonach Sie fragen möchten.

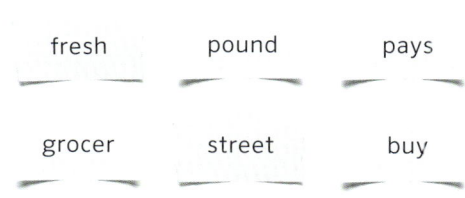

a 4 Orangen
b 1 Pfund rote Äpfel
c nach italienischem Kaffee fragen
d nach dem Preis fragen

a *I want to buy four oranges, please.*

b *Could I . . .*

c ....

d ....

3 Wie heißt das auf Englisch?

a *half*
halb

b
Dame

c
italienisch

d
viel

e
Entschuldigung!

f
Obst

g
Markt

h
kaufen

i
irgendwelche

j
Datum

Unbestimmte Mengenangaben

Um eine unbestimmte Menge oder Anzahl anzugeben, brauchen Sie im Englischen die Wörter some und any.

In <mark>Aussagesätzen</mark> steht normalerweise **some**.

I just want some grapes.

Ich möchte nur ein paar Trauben.

In <mark>Fragesätzen</mark> und <mark>verneinten</mark> Aussagesätzen steht **any**.

Have you got any grapes?
Haben Sie (irgendwelche) Trauben?

There aren't any grapes.
Es gibt keine Trauben.

Bestimmte Mengenangaben

Um eine bestimmte Menge anzugeben brauchen Sie die Präposition of.

A pound **of** **apples, please.**
Ein Pfund Äpfel, bitte.

Two **of** **those lovely oranges.**
Zwei von jenen schönen Orangen.

One **of** **my tyres is flat.**
Einer meiner Reifen ist platt.

Die Befehlsform

Die Befehlsform ist im Englischen ganz einfach: Sie stimmt mit der Grundform des Verbs überein.

Look over there.

Schau nach dort drüben.
Schaut nach dort drüben.
Schauen Sie nach dort drüben.

Es ist egal, ob Sie eine oder mehrere Personen zu etwas auffordern wollen.

Don't look over here.

Schau nicht nach hier.
Schaut nicht nach hier.
Schauen Sie nicht nach hier.

Sie verneinen den Imperativ, indem Sie **don't** vor das Verb setzen.

4

Ergänzen Sie *some* oder *any*.

a Have you got *any* .... oranges?

Yes, we've got .... lovely

oranges.

b Have you got .... coffee?

Yes, we've got .... good

Italian coffee.

c We haven't got .... new

projects this week.

d Paula would like to buy ....

fruit for Philip.

e Paula doesn't know ....

people in London.

f But she does! She knows ....

people in Islington.

5 👮

Übersetzen Sie die Sätze im Imperativ ins Englische.

a Genießen Sie Ihren Kaffee!

Enjoy your coffee!

b Kauf die Äpfel!

....

c Trinkt es nicht!

....

d Findet meinen Computer!

....

e Verlassen Sie das Haus nicht um acht

Uhr!

....

f Beantworte meine Frage!

....

6

Bringen Sie den Dialog zwischen Paula und dem Händler in die richtige Reihenfolge.

.... Paula: Yes. Could I have six, please?

And do you have any tomatoes?

.... Grocer: I'm fine too. What would you

like today?

.... Grocer: Of course. That's £2.50

altogether.

.... Paula: Yes, could I have a pound of

red apples, please?

1 Grocer: Good morning. How are you?

.... Paula: Do you have any eggs?

.... Grocer: I don't have any tomatoes

today. Would you like some apples?

.... Paula: I'm fine, thanks. How are you?

.... Grocer: Yes, I do. And they're very

fresh. Would you like some?

Mum — 11th November
Andy — 13th February
Me! — 15th May
John — 5th December
Hazel — 2nd March
Joyce — 21st August
Mr Butler — 17th May
Paula — ?

7

Dies ist Philips Geburtstags-kalender. Philip erzählt, wer wann Geburtstag hat. Fahren Sie fort.

Mum's birthday is on the eleventh of November.

Andy's

8

Verneinen Sie diese positiven Sätze. Achtung! Bei Verneinungen verwendet man *any* statt *some*.

---

a She has some fresh fruit.

She doesn't have any
fresh fruit.

b Paula buys some tea.

....

....

c They find some eggs at the market.

....

....

d Philip drinks some coffee in the canteen.

....

....

e We check some e-mails at the office.

....

....

f He understands some words.

....

....

9

◉ 046

Hören Sie die CD und reagieren Sie in den Sprechpausen. Verwenden Sie die folgenden Aussagen.

And a packet of tea, please.

Thank you very much, and goodbye.

I'd like some oranges, please.

Have you got any English apples?

Give me two pounds then.

How much are they?

6
IM RESTAURANT

In diesem Kapitel lernen Sie

Vorschläge
zu machen →

höflich Speisen
und Getränke
zu bestellen →

die Rechnung
zu bezahlen →

Wortschatz zum Dialog

◎ 047

restaurant
Restaurant

table
Tisch

window
Fenster

to sit
sitzen

menu
Speisekarte; Menü

soup
Suppe

starter
Vorspeise

salad
Salat

wine
Wein

over there
dort drüben

by
an, bei

perhaps
vielleicht

sir
mein Herr

there
dort, da

How about ...?
Wie wär's mit ...?

starter
Vorspeise

At Angelo's

⊚ 048 & 049

Paula and Philip are at an Italian restaurant in Islington.

PHILIP: A table for two, please.

WAITER: Over there, by the window, perhaps, sir?

Where would you like to sit, Paula?

PAULA: Yes, that table over there. It's nice there.

Here's the menu.

Thank you. What would you like, Paula?

How about a soup for starters. And then this salad looks very good.

Yes, good idea. And some wine for you? Red wine for me.

I like Italian red wine, too. How about some Chianti?

Can I help you, sir?

— Paula wants
☐ a soup ☐ baked beans.
— Paula and Philip like
☐ Spanish red wine
☐ Italian red wine.

◎ 051 & 052

PHILIP: We'd like the soup of the day to start with and then this salad here — for two. And a bottle of Chianti.

WAITER: The soup of the day, the salad and a bottle of Chianti. Anything else?

PAULA: And a bottle of water, please, and some bread.

Yes, madam. Thank you.

It's very international here. Look at those people over there. They're speaking German. And those two in the corner are talking Spanish.

Here you are, madam, sir. And some bread and a bottle of water.

Thank you very much. Enjoy your meal!

Can I have the bill, please?

No, Philip. I want to pay.

No, Paula, you're not paying! Well, let's go fifty-fifty. All right? Would you like to go to a pub?

No, not now, Philip. It's late. We've got a lot of work tomorrow.

— **The people in the restaurant are speaking**
 ☐ **Italian and French**
 ☐ **German and Spanish.**
— ☐ **Philip pays the bill.**
 ☐ **They go fifty-fifty.**

?

Wortschatz zum Dialog

◎ 050

to start
beginnen, anfangen

bottle
Flasche

to speak
sprechen

corner
Ecke

Spanish
spanisch
spenisch

bill
Rechnung

fifty-fifty
hier: halbe-halbe

late
spät

anything
irgendetwas

else
sonst

water
Wasser

bread
Brot

madam
meine Dame

international
international

Enjoy your meal!
Guten Appetit!

to enjoy
genießen

let's (let us)
lass(t) uns, lassen Sie uns

all right
in Ordnung

a lot of
viel(e)

tomorrow
morgen

Sprechstrategien

◎ 053

Sorry!
Verzeihung!

Do you speak German/ English?
Sprechen Sie Deutsch/ Englisch?

I didn't understand.
Ich habe nicht verstanden.

What is ...?
Was heißt ...?

Could you repeat that, please?
Könnten Sie das bitte wiederholen?

I understand.
Ich verstehe.

What does ... mean?
Was bedeutet ...?

How do you say ... in English?
Wie sagt man ... auf Englisch?

Could you speak more slowly, please?
Könnten Sie bitte langsamer sprechen?

1 Übersetzen Sie ins Englische.

a Bitte eine Flasche Wasser und etwas Brot.
A bottle of water and some bread, please.

b Könnten Sie das bitte wiederholen?

c Was bedeutet das?

d Wie sagt man das auf Englisch?

e Könnten Sie bitte langsamer sprechen?

2 Welche Form ist richtig? Unterstreichen Sie.

a I didn't understood / <u>understand</u> that.

b Do you speak / tell German?

c Where / Who is the station?

d Could you said / say that again?

e What's "Thank you" in / on Arabic?

f Sorry! / Pity! I didn't get that.

g Please repeat that / these.

h I don't know what you mean / mine.

3 Wie heißt das auf Englisch?

a *table*
Tisch

b
Rechnung

c
anfangen

d
Fenster

e
sitzen

f
Ecke

g
spät

h
Vorspeise

i
sprechen

j
Flasche

Die Personal-pronomen als Objekt

Personalpronomen können nicht nur als Subjekt (auf die Frage *wer?* oder *was?*), sondern auch als Objekt (*wen?*, *wem?* oder *was?*) verwendet werden.

SUBJEKT	OBJEKT	
I	**me**	*mich, mir*
you	**you**	*dich, dir/Sie, Ihnen*
he	**him**	*ihn, ihm*
she	**her**	*sie, ihr*
it	**it**	*es, ihm*
we	**us**	*uns*
you	**you**	*euch / Sie, Ihnen*
they	**them**	*sie, ihnen*

Red wine for me.
Rotwein für mich.

And some water for you?
Und (etwas) Wasser für dich?

Demonstrativ-
pronomen

This (Singular) und these (Plural) bezeichnen Gegenstände oder Personen, die in der Nähe sind; that (Singular) und those (Plural) Gegenstände oder Personen, die weiter weg sind.

I don't like this island.
Ich mag diese Insel nicht.

I would like to live on that island.
Ich würde gerne auf jener Insel leben.

But I'm not afraid of these rocks.
Aber ich habe keine Angst vor diesen Felsen.

I'm afraid of those sharks.
Ich habe Angst vor jenen Haien.

Das *present progressive*

Es gibt neben der einfachen Gegenwart noch eine zweite Verbform — die Verlaufsform der Gegenwart. Sie beschreibt, was gerade jetzt im Moment geschieht.

He is rowing on the river.

Er rudert (gerade) auf dem Fluss.

Das *present progressive* wird mit einer Form von **to be** und der Grundform des Verbs + **-ing** gebildet: **to speak — speaking**.

Dabei entfällt ein stummes -e am Wortende: **to have — having**.

Konsonanten, die nach einem kurzen betonten Vokal stehen, werden verdoppelt: **to sit — sitting** **to plan — planning**.

Fragen bilden Sie wie beim Verb **to be**: Vertauschen Sie Subjekt und Verb.

Are you cooking?
Kochst du gerade?

No, I'm fishing.
Nein, ich angle.

Yes, I am.
Ja.

No, I'm sleeping ★◉♩!!!
Nein, ich schlafe!!!

4

Was machen sie gerade?
Ergänzen Sie das passende
Verb in der Verlaufsform.

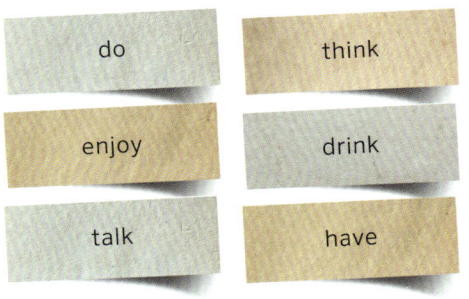

do	think
enjoy	drink
talk	have

a Philip is at work.

He *is drinking* .... coffee.

b Paula ....

lunch in the canteen.

c John ....

about a new project.

d I ....

my time in England.

e We ....

some work for Mr Butler.

f John and Hazel ....

about a computer problem.

5

*What are they doing at the
Italian restaurant?* Bilden Sie
Sätze in der Verlaufsform
der Gegenwart.

a Paula / Philip / sit / by the window

Paula and Philip are sitting

by the window.

b they / have / ravioli

....

....

c they / drink / red wine

....

....

d people / over there / speak / German

....

....

e people / in the corner / talk / Spanish

....

....

f waiter / come / this way

....

....

6

Welches Pronomen ist richtig? Kreuzen Sie an.

a Where's Philip? — I am calling
☐ his
☐ his
☐ him
now on my mobile phone.

b I would like to drink
☐ my
☐ me
☐ I
wine.

c Paula isn't here today. Where is
☐ she?
☐ her?
☐ he?

d What is
☐ you
☐ we
☐ your
soup like? It looks very good!

e They say they know
☐ we
☐ us
☐ our
from the office.

f Where are Paula and Philip going?
☐ Their
☐ Them
☐ They
are going to the pub.

7

⊚ 054

Hören Sie die Fragen in dem Restaurant und reagieren Sie mit den Vorgaben.

How about a starter?

I like Italian red wines.

No, not today. It's late.

Over there by the window.

This salad looks very good.

Yes, of course. Just a minute, please.

8

Setzen Sie *this, that, these* oder *those* ein.

Grocer: Would you like (a) *these* apples or (b) .... red apples over there?

Paula: Three of (c) .... apples here.

Grocer: And do you want (d) .... Italian coffee here or (e) .... coffee on the table there?

Paula: Well, I take (f) .... coffee over there. Please put* everything in (g) .... bag** here.

*to put — legen, stecken; **bag — Tasche

9

Reagieren Sie auf die Fragen entweder positiv (+) oder negativ (–).

a I'm drinking tea. And you? (+)

I'm drinking tea, too.

b I'm planning some new projects. What about you? (–)

....

c Philip is working at home. And you? (–)

....

d Paula is answering her e-mails. You? (+)

....

10

Unterstreichen Sie die richtige Form.

a I would like four of this/<u>these</u> lovely oranges, please.

b There are two of that/those computers in the office.

c This/That pub here has very good beer.

d How about these/those tables over there?

e We don't know this/these people.

f I am checking that/those e-mail again.

7

SEHENS-
WÜRDIGKEITEN

In diesem Kapitel lernen Sie

nach Informationen zu fragen →

die persönliche Meinung zu äußern →

eine Absicht auszudrücken →

Wortschatz zum Dialog

◉ 055

boat
Schiff, Boot
bout

to walk
(spazieren) gehen

ticket
Fahrkarte, Flugticket

queue
Reihe, Schlange
kju

to hurry
sich beeilen

inside
hinein; drinnen

fun
Spaß

trip
Fahrt, (kurze) Reise

Thames
Themse (Fluss)

Sunday
Sonntag

towards
nach, in Richtung

ticket office
Fahrkartenschalter

pier
Landungssteg

haven't you?
hier: nicht wahr?

must
müssen

open
offen

deck
(Schiffs)Deck

up
hinauf, nach oben

better
besser

seat
Sitz(platz)

A **boat trip** on the **Thames**

◎ 056 & 057

It is Sunday morning. Paula and Philip are walking towards Westminster Pier.

PAULA: Where's the ticket office?

PHILIP: It's over there by the pier. That's where we show our tickets. You've got your London Pass with you, haven't you? And I must buy a ticket. There's a queue. Come on. We must hurry.

On the boat

OK, where are we going to sit? There's an open deck or we can go inside.

Not inside. Let's go up to the open deck. We can see everything better there.

Look, there are two seats over there! This is going to be fun.

— The ticket office is by the pier.
  ☐ right ☐ wrong
— Philip has got a London Pass.
  ☐ right ☐ wrong

◎ 059 & 060

PAULA: So, what are we going to do?

PHILIP: Well, you must decide. I know all these places. There's the Tower of London, where they keep the Crown Jewels, but I think we can go there another day. There's St Paul's Cathedral with a fantastic view of London. We can get off at the Globe Theatre where there are excellent Shakespeare performances — but we needn't do everything in one day.

I'd like to go and see St Paul's Cathedral.

Fine. And after that we can just sit on the boat and look at all the famous sights.

I'm going to take some photos.

Aren't you going to take one of me?

May I? Stand over there with Big Ben behind you.

— **Paula wants to see the Globe Theatre.**
  ☐ right ☐ wrong
— **They keep the Crown Jewels in**
  ☐ St Paul's Cathedral ☐ the Tower.

?

Wortschatz zum Dialog

◎ 058

to **decide**
entscheiden
i ai

tower
Turm
au

cathedral
Dom, Kathedrale
i

to **get off**
aussteigen

famous
berühmt
ei

to **take a photo**
aufnehmen,
fotografieren

to **stand**
stehen; hier: sich stellen

place
ai
Ort

to **keep**
i
aufbewahren, behalten

Crown Jewels
juwels
Kronjuwelen

to **think**
denken

---

another
e
ein(e) andere(r, s)

fantastic
fantastisch

view
vju
Aussicht

theatre
te
Theater

excellent
hervorragend

performance
Aufführung

to **need**
i
brauchen

sight
ai
Sehenswürdigkeit

photo
ou
Foto

may
e
dürfen

behind
i ai
hinter; hinten

Präpositionen

◉ 061

in (London)
in (London)

at (the airport)
am (Flughafen)

after (midnight)
nach (Mitternacht)

at (noon)
um (12 Uhr mittags)

on/at (the corner)
an (der Ecke)

wann?

wo?

before (lunch)
vor (dem Mittagessen)

on (the bus)
im (Bus)

on (the internet)
im (Internet)

behind (you)
hinter (dir)

by (the tower)
neben (dem Turm)

in (a good mood)
in (guter Stimmung)

with (me)
mit (mir)

in (English)
auf (Englisch)

to (the office)
zum (Büro)

to (a pub)
zu (einer Kneipe)

wie?

woher?
wohin?

towards (the end)
zum (Ende) hin

for (lunch)
zum (Mittagessen)

from (Germany)
aus (Deutschland)

into (the box)
in (die Schachtel)

1 Setzen Sie eine passende Präposition ein. Es kann mehrere Lösungen geben.

at	in	on
to	for	from

a John is waiting _at_ the airport.

b Are you still _____ the hotel?

c She's _____ Manchester.

d The meeting is _____ the afternoon.

e Would you like to go out _____ dinner?

f I saw this _____ the Internet.

g I'm on my way _____ the office.

2 Sie unternehmen eine Bootsfahrt in London. Setzen Sie die fehlenden Wörter ein.

For a (a) _boat trip_ on the (b) _T_____ you first buy a (c) _t_____ at the ticket office. From the open (d) _d_____ of the boat you can then see Big Ben, St Paul's Cathedral and other (e) _f_____ sights. In the (f) _T_____ of London they keep the (g) _C_____ .

3 Wie heißt das auf Englisch?

a _tower_
Turm

b
sich beeilen

c
Spaß

d
aussteigen

e
stehen

f
Reihe, Schlange

g
Boot

h
sich entscheiden

i
berühmt

j
drinnen

Hilfsverben

Nach Wörtern wie **can**, **may** oder **must** steht immer ein Verb in der Grundform.

Diese sogenannten modalen Hilfsverben haben Sie bereits mit **can** und der Verneinung **can't** kennengelernt. Es gibt noch andere Modalverben, die ebenfalls verneint vorkommen können.

can	*können*
can't	*nicht können*
may	*dürfen*
may not	*nicht dürfen*
must	*müssen*
mustn't	*nicht dürfen (!)*
needn't	*nicht brauchen*

Can you help me?
Kannst du mir helfen?

I can't reach the pear.
Ich kann die Birne nicht erreichen.

He needn't count the sheep every day.
Er braucht die Schafe nicht jeden Tag zu zählen.

May I take a photo of you?

Darf ich ein Foto von dir machen?

No, you may not!

Nein, (das) darfst du nicht!

Beachten Sie, dass es keine Kurzform zu **may not** gibt.

She must hurry.

Sie muss sich beeilen.

But she mustn't go through the red light!

Aber sie darf die rote Ampel nicht überfahren!

Ganz wichtig: **mustn't** heißt nicht etwa *nicht müssen*, sondern *nicht dürfen*! Es drückt immer ein Verbot aus.

Nicht müssen heißt entweder **don't/doesn't have to** (siehe S. 194) oder **needn't**.

Die Zukunft mit *going to*

Sie verwenden **going to**, wenn Sie eine Absicht oder einen Plan für die Zukunft ausdrücken wollen. Nach **going to** steht immer ein Verb in der Grundform.

I'm going to win the race.
Ich werde das Rennen gewinnen.

I'm going to eat that cake.
Ich werde diesen Kuchen essen.

Das **going to**-Futur drückt auch aus, dass etwas in naher Zukunft ganz gewiss eintreten wird.

He is going to be late!
Er wird zu spät kommen!

4

Beantworten Sie die Fragen entweder positiv (+) oder negativ (–).

a I'm going to check my e-mails tomorrow morning. And what about Paula? (+)

Paula is going to check her e-mails tomorrow morning, too.

b Philip's going to take some photos tomorrow. And you? (–)

....

....

c They're going to meet some friends tomorrow evening. You and your friend? (–)

....

....

d Paula's going to stay at home on Saturday. And Philip? (+)

....

....

e We're going to see the sights on Sunday. And what about you? (+)

....

....

f I'm going to learn some Italian tomorrow. How about you? (–)

....

....

5

Pläne für die Zukunft: Bilden Sie Sätze mit *going to*.

a Sheila, Philip and Andy / have / breakfast.

Sheila, Philip and Andy are going to have breakfast.

b Paula and Philip / meet / ticket office.

....

....

c Philip / buy / ticket.

....

....

d They / sit / open deck.

....

....

e They / get off / St Paul's Cathedral.

....

....

f They / look at / Globe Theatre.

....

....

6

Lesen Sie den Text und ergänzen Sie die fehlenden Wörter.

The ticket (a) *office* is at Westminster Pier.
You can show your London Pass or buy a (b) ....
The boat has got an open (c) .... where you
can see everything or you can go (d) ....
But there are so many (e) .... to see.
There's the (f) .... of London where they
(g) .... the Crown Jewels. Then there's
St Paul's Cathedral with a fine (h) .... of
London. You can look at the Globe (i) ....
where there are excellent Shakespeare
(j) .... But you needn't do
(k) .... in one day. Come again another day!

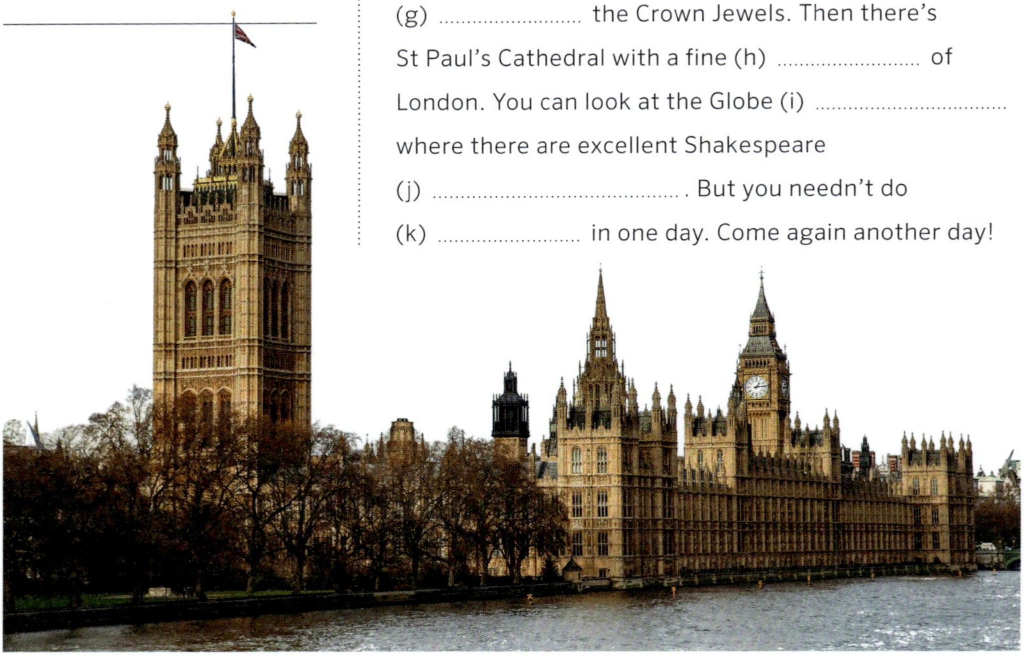

7

Ergänzen Sie die Sätze mit der englischen Entsprechung des deutschen Wortes in Klammern. Sprechen Sie die Sätze laut aus.

a We (*müssen*) *must* buy some bread for lunch.

b She (*nicht können*) .... find her ticket for the boat.

c You (*dürfen*) .... sit inside or on the open deck.

d They (*können*) .... go there another day.

e I (*nicht brauchen*) .... leave the house before eight o'clock.

f He (*nicht dürfen*) .... take any photos.

8

Welche Präposition passt? Kreuzen Sie an.

a Philip and Paula are sitting
☐ at ☐ before ☐ on
the boat.

b She goes for a walk
☐ before ☐ in ☐ towards
breakfast.

c What are you going to have
☐ to ☐ for ☐ on
lunch?

d The e-mail is
☐ from ☐ on ☐ in
English.

e Philip must go
☐ to ☐ on ☐ with
the office tomorrow.

f The ticket office is over there
☐ with ☐ for ☐ by
the pier.

g Sheila is not
☐ from ☐ to ☐ at
Germany.

h They're going to meet
☐ on ☐ in ☐ for
a restaurant.

9

Setzen Sie die passenden Hilfsverben ein.

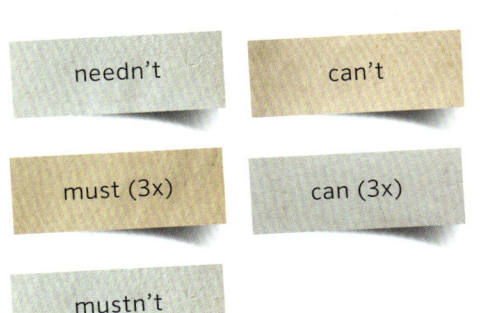

needn't   can't

must (3x)   can (3x)

mustn't

Philip (a) _must_ buy a ticket.
They (b) .... hurry because
there's a queue. They (c) .... be
late. On the boat they (d) ....
see everything better from the open deck.
Paula (e) .... decide about
the sights because Philip knows all the
places. They (f) .... see all the
sights in one day. They (g) ....
go to the Tower of London another day.
They (h) .... get off at the
Globe Theatre, but they (i) ....
do everything in one day.

8

SPORT UND FREIZEIT

**In diesem Kapitel
lernen Sie**

von Ihren Talenten
und Fähigkeiten
zu berichten →

über Freizeit-
beschäftigungen
zu sprechen →

regelmäßige und
gerade stattfindende
Tätigkeiten zu
unterscheiden →

Wortschatz zum Dialog

◎ 062

Weitere Vokabeln zu diesem Dialog finden Sie im Themenwortschatz auf Seite 118.

sports
Sport

afternoon
Nachmittag

sightseeing tour
Stadtrundfahrt

to **suppose**
vermuten, annehmen

to **play**
spielen

club
Klub, Verein

to **go for a walk**
einen Spaziergang machen

park
Park

Bingo
Bingo

back
zurück

myself
ich (selbst)

to **prefer**
vorziehen

as well
auch

(to be) good at
gut (sein) in

even
sogar

Do you like sports?

◎ 063 & 064

It's Sunday afternoon. Paula and Philip are back from their sightseeing tour. They're having tea with Sheila, Philip's mum, and Andy.

PAULA: What are the really typical English sports?

PHILIP: Cricket, I suppose. But I don't like playing cricket myself. I prefer rugby, but I'm too old for that now. I still play a bit of football. What about you, Paula, do you do any sports?

I play badminton for a club in Stuttgart.

Really? I can play badminton as well.

ANDY: But you're no good at badminton, Dad! Even I'm better!

And what do you do, Sheila?

SHEILA: Well, I really am too old for sports like that. I like going for walks in parks. And sometimes I play Bingo.

— Philip prefers
  ☐ cricket ☐ rugby.
— Sheila plays
  ☐ Bingo ☐ badminton.

◉ 066 & 067

PAULA: And what about you, Andy? Do you like sports?

ANDY: Skateboarding is best.

SHEILA: I think skateboarding is very dangerous. You can hurt yourself.

That's not true! There are lots of accidents when people play football, too.

And what about at school? You do a lot of sports at school in England, don't you?

We have football and cricket at school. That's OK, but I like skateboarding much better. And school is awful anyway. Although, at the moment I'm doing my homework together with a skateboarding friend. And my maths is getting better. She's really good at maths.

PHILIP: What's her name?

Oh, Dad. You're always asking questions!

— Andy likes
☐ football ☐ skateboarding best.
— Andy's friend is good at maths.
☐ right ☐ wrong

?

Wortschatz zum Dialog

◉ 065

Weitere Vokabeln zu diesem Dialog finden Sie im Themenwortschatz auf Seite 118.

skateboarding
Skateboardfahren

dangerous
gefährlich

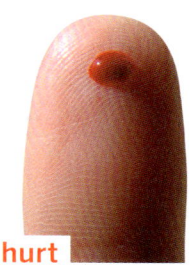

to **hurt**
verletzen

lots of
viele

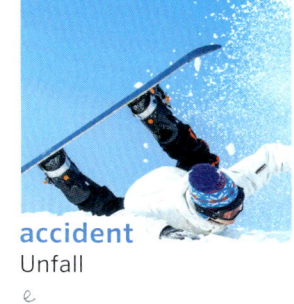

accident
Unfall

homework
Hausaufgaben

together
zusammen

maths
Mathe

best
beste(r, s); am besten

yourself
dich (selbst)

true
wahr

don't you?
hier: nicht wahr?

to **like ... better**
... lieber mögen

anyway
ohnehin; wie auch immer

although
obwohl

at the moment
im Moment

name
Name

question
Frage

Sportarten

◉ 068

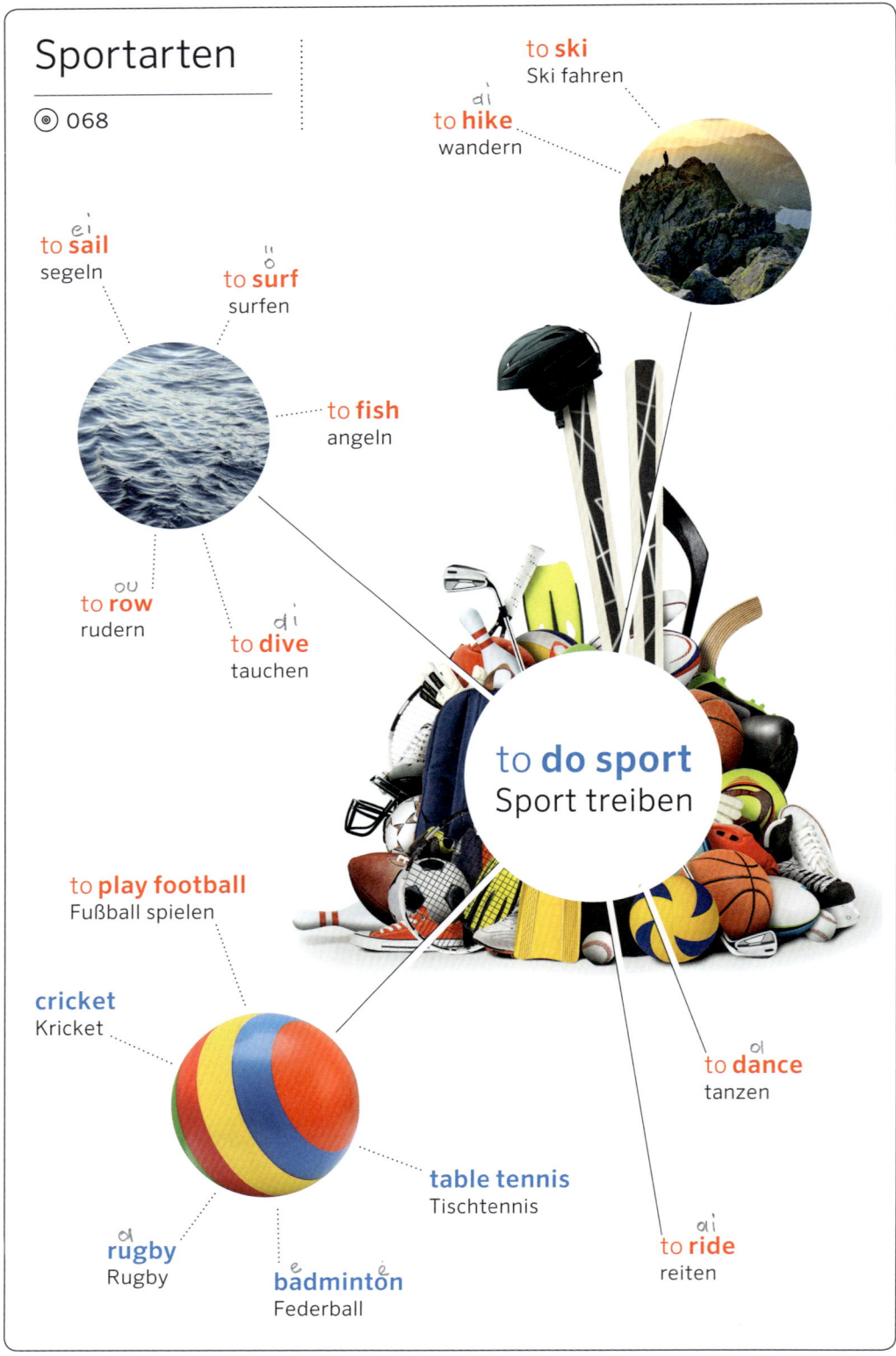

to **ski**
Ski fahren

to **hike**
wandern

to **sail**
segeln

to **surf**
surfen

to **fish**
angeln

to **row**
rudern

to **dive**
tauchen

to **do sport**
Sport treiben

to **play football**
Fußball spielen

cricket
Kricket

to **dance**
tanzen

table tennis
Tischtennis

to **ride**
reiten

rugby
Rugby

badminton
Federball

1 Verbinden Sie das Verb mit der passenden Freizeitaktivität.

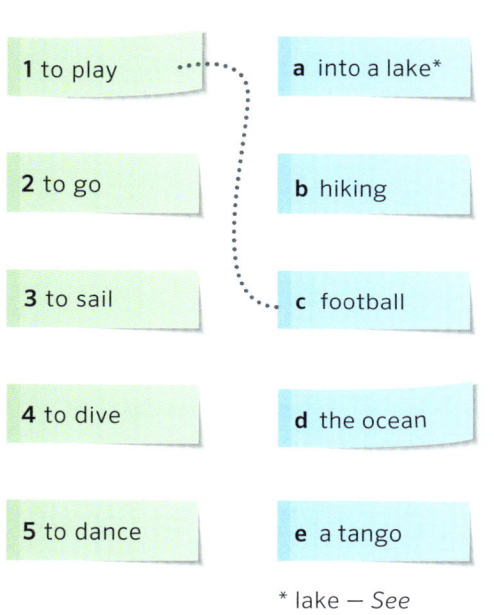

1 to play

2 to go

3 to sail

4 to dive

5 to dance

a into a lake*

b hiking

c football

d the ocean

e a tango

* lake – *See*

2 Geben Sie drei Sport-arten an, die Sie mögen, und drei, die Sie nicht mögen.

a I like:

....

....

....

b I don't like:

....

....

....

3 Wie heißt das auf Englisch?

a *homework*
Hausaufgaben

c ....
vermuten

e ....
zusammen

h ....
Klub, Verein

b ....
Nachmittag

d ....
Unfall

f ....
spielen

i ....
gefährlich

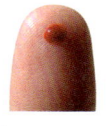

g ....
verletzen

j ....
viele

Das Reflexivpronomen

Mit dem rückbezüglichen Fürwort **-self/-selves** *(sich selbst)* können Sie das Subjekt oder Objekt eines Satzes betonen.

Auch viele Verben stehen mit dem Pronomen **-self/-selves**:

to hurt oneself
sich verletzen

to enjoy oneself
sich amüsieren

You can hurt yourself.
Du kannst dich verletzen.

I can do it myself.
Ich kann es selbst.

Manchmal ist ein Verb im Englischen nicht reflexiv, im Deutschen aber schon, z. B. **to meet** — *sich treffen*

We meet at the bus stop.
Wir treffen uns an der Bushaltestelle.

I	myself
you	yourself
he	himself
she	herself
it	itself
we	ourselves
you	yourselves
they	themselves

Das *simple present* und das *present progressive*

Die einfache Gegenwart und die Verlaufsform haben unterschiedliche Funktionen.

Die einfache Gegenwart (*simple present*) beschreibt Handlungen, die <mark>regelmäßig ausgeführt werden</mark>, oft in Verbindung mit den Häufigkeitsadverbien (*always, usually, often, sometimes, never;* siehe S. 33).

Die Verlaufsform der Gegenwart (*present progressive*) beschreibt Handlungen, die <mark>gerade ablaufen und noch nicht abgeschlossen sind</mark>.

In the morning Robert always sits on the riverbank.

Morgens sitzt Robert immer am Flussufer.

Today Steven is rowing on the river.

Heute rudert Steven auf dem Fluss.

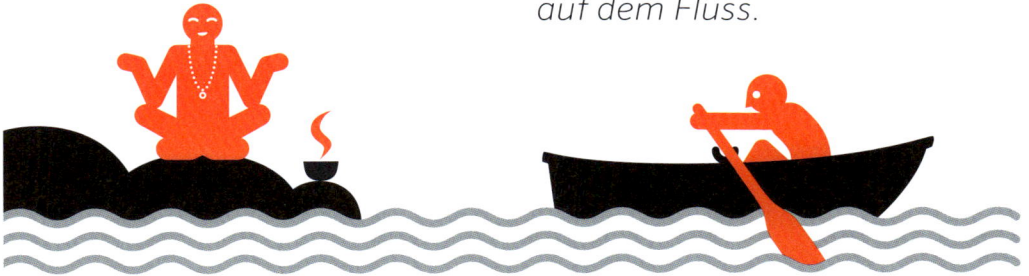

Achtung: <mark>Ausnahmsweise</mark> kann *always* auch mit der <mark>Verlaufsform</mark> benutzt werden. Es drückt dann aus, dass man <mark>verärgert</mark> ist.

You're always snoring at night!

Immer schnarchst du in der Nacht!

Das Gerund (I)

Aus einem <mark>Verb wird</mark> ein <mark>Substantiv</mark>, wenn Sie die Endung **-ing** an die Grundform anhängen.

Diese Form heißt Gerund. Sie kann sowohl Subjekt als auch Objekt im Satz sein. Als Objekt steht das Gerund z.B. nach Verben wie **enjoy** *Freude haben an, gerne tun* oder **like** *mögen, gerne haben*.

Skateboarding is best.
Skateboarden ist das Beste.

I **like** cooking.
Ich mag Kochen. (= Ich koche gerne.)

I don't **like** playing cricket.
Ich spiele nicht gerne Kricket.

Cooking is fun.
Kochen macht Spaß.

4 Ergänzen Sie die Verben. Entscheiden Sie, ob die Tätigkeit gerade stattfindet oder ob sie regelmäßig geschieht.

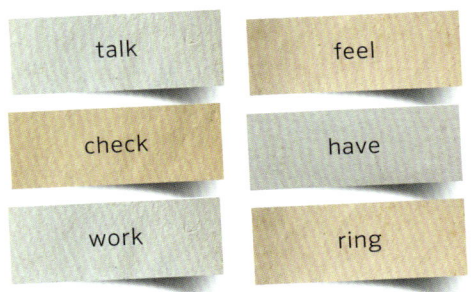

talk   feel
check   have
work   ring

a Paula usually *works* in Stuttgart but now she *is working* in London.

b She always .... her e-mails in the morning but today she .... her e-mails in the afternoon.

c The phone .... now. It often .... and ....

d They .... lunch in a pub today. Usually they .... lunch in the canteen.

e Philip .... to his boss every morning, but at the moment he .... to his colleagues.

f Sheila often .... lonely. Today she .... very lonely.

5 Setzen Sie das passende Reflexivpronomen ein.

a Sheila always enjoys *herself* at Bingo.

b They like to cook their meals ....

c The pub .... is nice but the beer is not good.

d Philip doesn't like playing cricket ....

e I don't know how to do that ....

f Paula and Philip are enjoying .... on the boat trip.

g Andy, don't hurt .... when you're skateboarding!

6   Welche Übersetzung passt?

1 They are enjoying themselves at the pub.

2 She doesn't like rugby herself.

3 You can hurt yourself.

4 I prefer coffee myself.

5 He likes playing cricket himself.

a Ich persönlich ziehe Kaffee vor.

b Du kannst dich verletzen.

c Er persönlich spielt gern Kricket.

d Sie amüsieren sich in der Kneipe.

e Sie persönlich mag kein Rugby.

7   Lesen Sie den Text rechts. Ordnen Sie alle darin vorkommenden Verben einer Kategorie zu.

Today Philip is playing cricket with his colleagues. They always start at ten o'clock in the park. Philip usually drinks some coffee first. Now he is phoning Paula. She is enjoying herself on a sightseeing tour this morning. She likes looking at the famous sights. At the moment she is taking a photo of Big Ben.

a simple present:

....

....

....

b present progressive:

is playing

....

....

....

8

⊚ 069

Hören Sie die Fragen von der CD und beantworten Sie sie mit den Vorgaben. Nach der Pause hören Sie die Antwort.

We have football and cricket at school.

I can play badminton, but not very well.

There's a halfpipe not far from here.

Football and cricket, I suppose.

I like going for walks and sometimes I play Bingo.

Skateboarding is best.

9

Füllen Sie das Kreuzworträtsel aus. Wie lautet das Lösungswort?

a Sheila likes going for .....
b first, second, ...
c Paula is from .....
d ..... and eggs for breakfast?
e May, June, ...
f fifty, sixty, ...
g Mum and .....
h Let's sit on ..... seats over there.
i A ..... of apples, please.

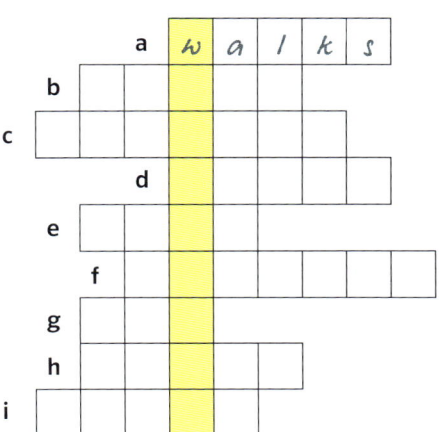

9

NEUE FREUND-SCHAFTEN

**In diesem Kapitel
lernen Sie**

jemanden oder etwas
zu beschreiben →

etwas miteinander
zu vergleichen →

jemanden zu etwas
aufzufordern →

Wortschatz zum Dialog

◉ 070

Weitere Vokabeln zu diesem Dialog finden Sie im Themenwortschatz auf Seite 132.

crazy
verrückt
kraisi

quiet
ruhig, leise
k reit

music
Musik

loud
laut
laud

to pour out
eingießen

to turn down
herunterdrehen,
leiser stellen

downstairs
unten (im Haus)

to enjoy
genießen
in

household
Haushalt

end
Ende

hard
hart, schwer

candlelit
Kerzenlicht-

dinner
Abendessen

to put
setzen, stellen, legen

to have a word with sb.
mit jdm. (ein Wörtchen) reden

than
als

usual *juschual*
üblich, gewöhnlich

take it easy
nimm's leicht

A crazy household

◉ 071 & 072

Friday evening — the end of a hard week at work. Philip and Paula are planning a quiet candlelit dinner.

PHILIP: Andy's music gets louder and louder every day! Would you put the meal on the table, please, and pour out the wine? I want to go upstairs and have a word with Andy. (...) Andy! Oh, hello.

ANDY: Hi, Dad. Um, this is Lisa.

LISA: Hello, Mr Elton. We're doing our maths homework together.

Can't you turn that music down a bit, Andy? Paula and I are having a meal downstairs.

OK, Dad. But it's not louder than usual!

Downstairs.

PAULA: Everything's on the table. That's much better now. The music is quieter. Take it easy and enjoy your meal.

— Andy and Lisa are
☐ downstairs ☐ upstairs.
— They are doing their
☐ maths homework
☐ English homework.

◎ 074 & 075

PHILIP: Lisa seems very nice ... nicer than his last girlfriend. But she's got two piercings in her nose. I really don't know! Anyway, what are you doing this weekend, Paula?

PAULA: Tomorrow we're going to the cinema together. Don't forget that!

No, I won't. Oh, that's Mum coming in! No peace for us here. And she's got someone with her.

SHEILA: Hello, Paula, hello, Philip. Oh, you're having dinner. Lovely. This is Mahmoud, Mahmoud Aziz, a friend. These flowers are from him — the loveliest, biggest flowers in the shop. And we've got an Indian takeaway, so we can all eat together.

Nice to meet you, Mr Aziz. They really are lovely flowers.

— Lisa is ☐ nicer ☐ quieter than Andy's last girlfriend.
— Sheila and Mahmoud have got an ☐ Italian ☐ Indian takeaway.

Wortschatz zum Dialog

◉ 073

Weitere Vokabeln zu diesem Dialog finden Sie im Themenwortschatz auf Seite 132.

girlfriend
Freundin

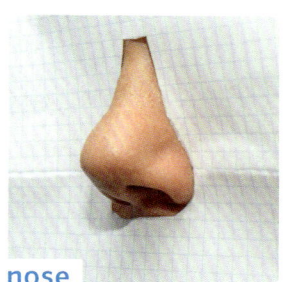

nose
Nase
nous

cinema
Kino

to forget
vergessen

flower
Blume
flauer

shop
Geschäft

Indian
indisch

to eat
essen

---

to seem
scheinen

weekend
Wochenende

**won't
(= will not)**
nicht werden

peace
Frieden, hier: Ruhe

someone
irgendjemand

big
groß

Indian
Inder(in)

takeaway
Essen zum Mitnehmen;
Imbissbude

Wochen- und Feiertage

◎ 076

SUNDAY
MONDAY
TUESDAY
PLANNER & CALENDAR
WEDNESDAY **THURSDAY**
FRIDA
SATU

Sunday
Sonntag

Monday
Montag

Tuesday
Dienstag

Wednesday
Mittwoch

Thursday
Donnerstag

Friday
Freitag

Saturday
Samstag

Der SONNTAG ist der erste Tag
der Woche. Beachten Sie, dass
alle Wochentage im Englischen
immer großgeschrieben werden.

working day
Werktag

weekend
Wochenende

holiday
Feiertag

Easter
Ostern

Christmas Eve
Weihnachtsabend

New Year's Eve
Silvester

1 Was fehlt hier? Ergänzen Sie.

a _Sunday_ ....
is the first day of the week.

b ....
is the eighth month of the year.

c ....
is the third day of the week.

d ....
is the tenth month of the year.

e ....
is the second day of the week.

f ....
is the fifth month of the year.

g ....
is the sixth day of the week.

2 Finden Sie die englische Entsprechung.

a Neujahr ········

b Ostern

c Wochenende

d Silvester

e Heiligabend

f Weihnachten

1 New Year's Eve

2 Christmas

3 New Year's Day

4 Christmas Eve

5 weekend

6 Easter

3 Wie heißt das auf Englisch?

a _to eat_
essen

b
laut

c
unten (im Haus)

d
vergessen

e
eingießen

f
Blume

g
leise

h
Nase

i
genießen

j
verrückt

Die Steigerung der Adjektive (I)

Viele englische Adjektive werden durch Anhängen von -er/-est gesteigert. Das gilt für alle einsilbigen Adjektive und die zweisilbigen auf -y.

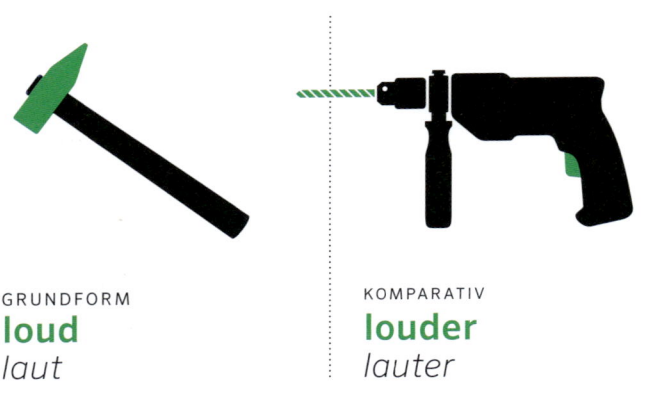

GRUNDFORM
loud
laut

KOMPARATIV
louder
lauter

SUPERLATIV
(the) **loudest**
*(der/die/das)
lauteste*

Beachten Sie, dass ein einzelner Konsonant nach einem kurzen Vokal verdoppelt wird.	**big** *groß*	**bigger** *größer*	(the) **biggest** *(der/die/das) größte*
Ein nicht gesprochenes -e am Wortende entfällt.	**nice** *nett*	**nicer** *netter*	(the) **nicest** *(der/die/das) netteste*
Endet ein Adjektiv auf Konsonant und -y, wird das -y vor der Endung -er/-est zu -i-.	**lovely** *hübsch*	**lovelier** *hübscher*	(the) **loveliest** *(der/die/das) hübscheste*

Merken Sie sich die folgenden <mark>unregelmäßigen Steigerungen</mark> gut — sie kommen häufig vor!

good
gut

better
besser

(the) **best**
(der/die/das) beste

bad
schlecht

worse
schlechter

(the) **worst**
(der/die/das) schlechteste

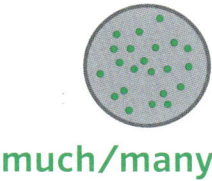

much/many
viel(e)

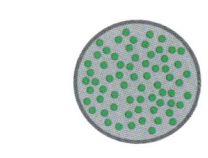

more
mehr

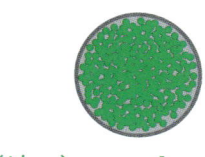

(the) **most**
(der/die/das) meiste

Vergleiche

Für einen Vergleich verwenden Sie das Wort **than** (*als*) mit dem Adjektiv im Komparativ.

My bicycle is bigger than your bicycle.
Mein Fahrrad ist größer als dein Fahrrad.

Das *present progressive* mit zukünftiger Bedeutung

Die Verlaufsform der Gegenwart kann auch ausdrücken, dass etwas vereinbart oder geplant ist. Meist wird durch eine Zeitangabe klar, dass die Zukunft gemeint ist.

Jack is flying to Hawaii on Saturday.
Jack fliegt am Samstag nach Hawaii.

Achtung: Die Zeitangabe steht im Englischen entweder am Satzanfang oder am Satzende, nie in der Mitte wie im Deutschen!

4

Welche Form des Adjektivs ist richtig? Kreuzen Sie an.

a St Paul's is not the
☐ old ☐ older ☐ oldest
cathedral in England.

b My boat is
☐ big ☐ bigger ☐ biggest
than your boat.

c Andy's music is very
☐ loud ☐ louder ☐ loudest
this evening.

d These apples are the
☐ fresh ☐ fresher ☐ freshest
on the market.

e This soup is
☐ good ☐ better ☐ best
than that soup.

f I think Sheila's idea is the
☐ crazy ☐ crazier ☐ craziest.

g We are going for a
☐ nice ☐ nicer ☐ nicest
walk tomorrow.

h This restaurant is
☐ quiet ☐ quieter ☐ quietest
than that pub.

5

◎ 077

Hören Sie die CD und notieren Sie, was Andy und Lisa an welchem Wochentag vorhaben.

a Wochentag   Aktivität
   Friday   *cinema*

b Wochentag   Aktivität

c Wochentag   Aktivität

d Wochentag   Aktivität

6

Setzen Sie das passende Adjektiv in der richtigen Form ein.

big

quiet

good

loud

nice

lovely

a Andy's music is much _louder_ today.

b Philip talks to Andy. The music is .... now.

c Lisa is .... than Andy's last girlfriend.

d Paula is .... at badminton than Philip.

e Sheila has got the .... flowers from the flower shop.

f They are also the .... flowers.

7

Bilden Sie Sätze nach dem Muster. Sprechen Sie erst den Satz und schreiben Sie ihn dann auf. Die Zeitangabe kann entweder am Satzanfang oder am Satzende stehen.

a Thursday / he / work later than usual
(On Thursday) He is working later than usual (on Thursday).

b Friday / they / go to the cinema
....
....
....

c Saturday / we / go shopping at one of the markets
....
....
....

d Sunday / she / go for a walk in one of the parks
....
....
....

e Monday / I / have lunch with Mr Butler
....
....
....

f Tuesday / Lisa / help Andy with his homework
....
....
....

g Wednesday / they / meet at the Globe Theatre
....
....
....

8

Beantworten Sie mündlich die Fragen zu Philips Woche mit dem *present progressive* mit zukünftiger Bedeutung.

a Was macht Philip am Sonntag um 10 Uhr?

b Wo wird er am Freitagabend sein?

c Was macht er am Donnerstag um 11 Uhr?

d Was macht Philip am Dienstag?

e Was macht er am Samstagabend?

f Was macht Philip am Freitagnachmittag?

g Was macht er am Sonntagabend?

Month	1	2	3	4	5	6	7	8	9	10	11	12				
3 monday montag / lundi	**4** tuesday dienstag / mardi	**5** wednesday mittwoch / mercredi	**6** thursday donnerstag / jeudi	**7** friday freitag / vendredi	**8** saturday samstag / samedi	**9** sunday sonntag / dimanche
	Buy new computer		11 am Meeting with Joyce Marlow 2 pm Meeting with Mr Butler	3 pm Show Paula offices Pub with Andy	1 pm St Paul's Cathedral. Paula 8 pm Dinner with Paula. Krishna's Restaurant	10 am Football. Blackwood Park Call Aunt Rosie

10

ALLTAGS-PFLICHTEN

**In diesem Kapitel
lernen Sie**

über Vergangenes
zu sprechen →

sich über alltäg-
liche Dinge aus-
zutauschen →

Vorlieben und Abnei-
gungen zu äußern →

Wortschatz zum Dialog

◉ 078

mess
Unordnung, Chaos

breakfast
Frühstück

to **listen to**
zuhören, anhören

concert
Konzert

to **watch**
anschauen, zusehen

film
Film

chore
Hausarbeit

house
Haus

out
hinaus; draußen

who
wer

yesterday
gestern

to **spend**
verbringen; ausgeben

at her place
bei ihr zu Hause

sports centre
Sportcenter

What a **mess!**

◎ 079 & 080

Philip, Sheila and Andy are sitting at
breakfast on Saturday morning.

SHEILA: I was out with Mahmoud
yesterday evening. We listened
to a concert in the park.

PHILIP: And what about you,
Andy?

ANDY: I met Lisa and we
watched a film at her place.
And you, Dad?

Well, I went to the sports
centre with Paula and we played
badminton.

That's all very nice, but I want
to know who is going to do
the most boring chores in this
house.

You know that I've got lots of
work, Mum. I haven't got time.

Oh yes, Dad, and what
about me? I've got school and
homework and I want to spend
time with my friends, too.

— Sheila and Mahmoud
  ☐ went to a restaurant
  ☐ listened to a concert.
— Philip played
  ☐ football with Andy
  ☐ badminton with Paula.

◉ 082 & 083

SHEILA: And you may not realize it, you two young men, but even at my age I've got lots of things to do. Andy, when was the last time you tidied up your room?

ANDY: Last week!

Well, you can tidy it up again this weekend. It's an awful mess. At least do it before Lisa comes to see you.

Ugh, OK, Gran.

And Philip, how about a good idea from your mum: Paula's unhappy with her B&B. She's got the most uncomfortable room in the house. I was there. Why doesn't she come and live with us? Our attic room is nice and big and much more attractive than her little room.

PHILIP: Oh, Mum. Let me decide about things like that.

— Sheila
  ☐ hasn't got anything to do
  ☐ has got lots of things to do.
— Andy tidied up his room
  ☐ last week ☐ yesterday.

Wortschatz zum Dialog

◎ 081

young
jung
ol

man *(Pl men)*
Mann
e

woman *(Pl women)*
Frau
u   *i*

to **tidy up**
aufräumen
aldi

tidy
ordentlich, aufgeräumt
taidi

again
noch einmal, wieder
c e

gran
Oma
e

unhappy
unglücklich
ol

attic
Dachboden
e

you may not realize it, but ...
es mag euch nicht bewusst sein, aber ...
ed dis

to **realize**
wahrnehmen; begreifen

age
Alter
e

time
hier: Mal
i

at least
wenigstens, zumindest

attractive
attraktiv

to **let**
lassen

145

Das simple past der unregelmäßigen Verben

◎ 084

to buy → bought
kaufen   *ougt*
         a

to sit → sat
sitzen   *e*
         a

to put → put
setzen, stellen, legen

to drink → drank
trinken   *e*

to take → took
nehmen; bringen   *u*

to think → thought
denken   *thoght*

to stand → stood
stehen   *u*

to speak → spoke
sprechen   *ouk*

to eat → ate
essen   *ait*

to come → came
kommen   *caim*
         a

to find → found
finden   *found*
         ai
         ai

to **do → did**
tun

to **feel → felt**
fühlen   *foult*

to **forget → forgot**
vergessen

to **get → got**
holen; werden

to **go → went**
gehen, fahren

to **have → had**
haben

to **hear → heard**
hören

to **hurt → hurt**
verletzen

to **keep → kept**
aufbewahren,
behalten

to **know → knew**   *njuw*
kennen, wissen

to **let → let**
lassen

to **meet → met**
treffen, kennen-
lernen

to **pay → paid**
bezahlen

to **ring → rang**
klingeln

to **say → said**
sagen

to **see → saw**   *sow*
sehen

to **spend → spent**
verbringen; ausgeben

to **understand
→ understood**
verstehen

Das *simple past* von *to be*

◎ 085

I **was**
ich war

you **were**
du warst/Sie waren

he/she/it **was**
er/sie/es war

we **were**
wir waren

you **were**
ihr wart/Sie waren

they **were**
sie waren

I **was** there.
Ich war dort.

Were you late?
Warst du zu spät?

They **weren't** at
home yesterday.
Sie waren gestern
nicht zu Hause.

1 Setzen Sie die richtige Form des Verbs im *simple past* ein.

a Yesterday I ___bought___ (buy) a new car*.

b We .... (go) to the zoo last week.

c She .... (drink) four cups** of tea.

d I .... (find) it on the Internet.

e He .... (take) the CDs home.

f I .... (meet) them last Monday.

g They .... (get) home late.

h I .... (do) everything I could.

*car — *Auto;* **cup — *Tasse*

2 Welches Wort passt nicht in die Reihe? Kreuzen Sie an.

a ☐ excellent
☐ fantastic
☐ terrible

d ☐ dinner
☐ lunch
☐ takeaway

b ☐ September
☐ Sunday
☐ Saturday

e ☐ theatre
☐ office
☐ cinema

c ☐ concert
☐ yesterday
☐ today

f ☐ woman
☐ age
☐ man

3 Wie heißt das auf Englisch?

a
___concert___
Konzert

c
aufräumen

e
wieder

h
anschauen

b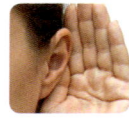
Frau

d
zuhören

f
Oma

i
Unordnung

g
unglücklich

j
jung

Das *simple past*

Diese Zeitform, die einfache Vergangenheit, wird bei Handlungen verwendet, die <mark>abgeschlossen</mark> sind und keine Auswirkung mehr auf die Gegenwart haben.

He pushed the trolley to the counter.
Er schob den Einkaufswagen zur Theke.

DAS SIMPLE PAST DER REGELMÄSSIGEN VERBEN	GRUNDFORM	SIMPLE PAST
Meist wird einfach **-ed** an die Grundform angehängt.	to **push** *schieben*	push**ed**
Bei einem nicht gesprochenen **-e** am Wortende wird nur **-d** angehängt.	to **like** *mögen*	like**d**
Ein Endkonsonant wird nach kurzem betontem Vokal verdoppelt.	to **prefer** *bevorzugen*	prefer**red**
Steht **-y** nach einem Konsonant, wird es zu **-ied**.	to **try** *versuchen*	tr**ied**
Steht **-y** nach einem Vokal, bleibt es unverändert.	to **play** *spielen*	play**ed**

Die Steigerung der Adjektive (II)

werden durch das Voranstellen von **more** und **most** gesteigert.

Ausgenommen sind auf **-y** endende zweisilbige Adjektive, die durch Anhängen von **-er** und **-est** gesteigert werden (siehe S. 134).

GRUNDFORM
boring
langweilig

KOMPARATIV
more boring
langweiliger

SUPERLATIV
(the) **most boring**
(der/die/das) langweiligste

The attic room is more attractive than her little room.
Die Mansarde ist attraktiver als ihr kleines Zimmer.

Who is going to do the most boring chores?
Wer wird die langweiligsten Hausarbeiten machen?

4

Wie lauten diese Sätze in der Vergangenheit? Schreiben Sie nur die Verben auf.

a Sheila and Mahmoud talk about many things.
talked

b They enjoy the walk.
....

c They prefer a café to an expensive restaurant.
....

d They like the coffee there.
....

e Sheila plays Bingo.
....

f She enjoys it very much.
....

g The next week they have coffee again.
....

h They go for a walk in the park.
....

i After that they do some shopping at a street market.
....

5

Ergänzen Sie die passende Adjektivform. Es kann mehrere Möglichkeiten geben.

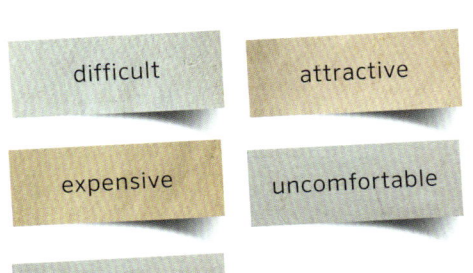

difficult

attractive

expensive

uncomfortable

depressed

a My room is the *most uncomfortable/ attractive* room in the house.

b This is the .... flat in the street.

c This project is .... than the project last week.

d And this job is .... than the other job.

e Last weekend I was .... than today.

6

◉ 086

Hören Sie das Gespräch zwischen Lisa und ihrer Mutter. Ergänzen Sie Lisas Aussagen.

Last week. OK, Mum, I can tidy it up a bit this evening.

Yes, Mum. Of course, Mum. He's coming tomorrow.

I just haven't got the time, Mum.

That's a better idea. I like cooking.

Well, I could help you on Saturday.

And I don't want you to tidy up my things!

7

Welches Wort passt zu dem Substantiv? Tragen Sie es ein.

a An *awful* .... mess.

anyway / alright / awful

b A .... meeting.

wine / wonderful / window

c An .... restaurant.

interest / Italian / invite

d A .... pub.

quiet / quite / question

e A .... colleague.

terrible / today / towards

f An .... market.

often / open / office

g .... food.

surprised / school / Spanish

8

Die Tabelle enthält einige englische Adjektive in der Grundform und in den Steigerungen Komparativ und Superlativ. Ergänzen Sie die fehlenden Formen.

GRUNDFORM	KOMPARATIV	SUPERLATIV
late	later	*latest*
		most boring
typical		
	worse	
great		
	more difficult	
		youngest
good		

11 FAMILIENLEBEN

**In diesem Kapitel
lernen Sie**

kleine Meinungs-
verschiedenheiten
auszutragen →

Zeitangaben
und Jahreszahlen
zu verstehen →

sich über Ereignisse
in der Vergangenheit
auszutauschen →

Wortschatz zum Dialog

◎ 087

meat
Fleisch

potato(es)
Kartoffel(n)

soft
weich

maybe
vielleicht

to cook
kochen

to learn
lernen, erfahren

vegetables
Gemüse

tough
zäh

answer
Antwort

bad
schlecht

food
Essen

speciality
Spezialität

something
(irgend)etwas

should
sollte(n)

roast
Braten

beef
Rindfleisch

Yorkshire pudding
(Beilage zu Fleischgerichten)

lamb
Lamm(fleisch)

pork
Schweinefleisch

roast potatoes
Bratkartoffeln

various
verschieden(e)

Sunday lunch

◉ 088 & 089

ANDY: Hey, Dad. This meat is tough and the potatoes are too soft.

PHILIP: Well, why don't you do the cooking then?

No time, Dad!

Always the same old answer!

PAULA: I could help you with the cooking. I'm not a bad cook.

Hey, that's a great idea. What's German food like?

Very good, but I only know specialities from the south of Germany.

So, maybe you could cook us something German. Please!

PHILIP: Paula's here to learn about England. Maybe she should learn about the English Sunday roast. Beef with Yorkshire pudding, lamb or pork with roast potatoes and various vegetables. Like in the good old days.

— The meat is good.
☐ right ☐ wrong
— Paula is a bad cook.
☐ right ☐ wrong

◉ 091 & 092

PAULA: What was it like when you were young, Sheila?

SHEILA: Ah yes, the good old days. I was born in 1940. We all lived in the country.

And when did you move to Islington?

My dad bought the house here in 1947. It was very different then. Houses were much cheaper. It was more like a village.

And why did you stay here? Why didn't you go back to the country?

Because I like Islington. It's my home. But a house and a garden are a lot of work.

Well, I like it very much here. And I think London is a wonderful city. There are so many things to see and do.

— Sheila moved to Islington in 1947. ☐ right ☐ wrong
— Sheila wants to go back to the country. ☐ right ☐ wrong

?

Wortschatz zum Dialog

◎ 090

to **be born**
geboren werden

country
Land

to **move**
bewegen;
hier: umziehen
mouv

cheap
billig
tschip

village
Dorf ,tsch

home
Zuhause

garden
Garten

wonderful
wundervoll

city
Stadt

to **stay**
bleiben

because
weil

Länder und Nationalitäten

◎ 093

north
Norden

west
Westen

east
Osten

south
Süden

United States
Vereinigte Staaten

American
amerikanisch

Great Britain
Großbritannien

British
britisch

Ireland
Irland

Irish
irisch

Germany
Deutschland

German
deutsch

France
Frankreich

French
französisch

Switzerland
Schweiz

Swiss
schweizerisch

Austria
Österreich

Austrian
österreichisch

Spain
Spanien

Spanish
spanisch

Portugal
Portugal

Portuguese
portugiesisch

Italy
Italien

Italian
italienisch

1 Geben Sie die Sprache an, die man in diesen Ländern hauptsächlich spricht.

a Germany
German

e Austria

b Spain

f Italy

c France

g Portugal

d Ireland

h Great Britain

2 Wo liegen die folgenden Länder? Tragen Sie die Himmelsrichtung ein.

a France is *west* of Germany.

b Spain is of France.

c England is of Ireland.

d Switzerland is of Germany.

e Switzerland is of Italy.

f Austria is of Switzerland.

g Portugal is of Spain.

h France is of Spain.

3 Wie heißt das auf Englisch?

a *vegetables*
Gemüse

c
Dorf

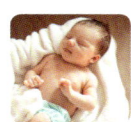

e
geboren werden

h
Kartoffeln

b
billig

d
Garten

f
kochen

i
umziehen

g
Stadt

j
wundervoll

Verneinung, Frage und Kurzantwort im *simple past*

Für eine <mark>Verneinung</mark> in der einfachen Vergangenheit wird in der Regel das *simple past* von **don't/doesn't** vor die Grundform des Vollverbs gestellt. Es lautet immer **didn't** (**did not**).

I **didn't like** the soup.
Ich mochte die Suppe nicht.

She went **to the theatre.**
Sie ging ins Theater.

She didn't go **to the theatre.**
Sie ging nicht ins Theater.

He liked **meat.**
Er mochte Fleisch.

He didn't like **tomatoes.**
Er mochte keine Tomaten.

Fragen, die Vollverben enthalten,
bilden Sie mit did/didn't.

*Mochtest
du den
Umzug?*

Mit did/didn't bilden Sie auch
Kurzantworten.

*Ja, ich
mochte
ihn.*

*Nein, ich
mochte
ihn nicht.*

Achtung: In Sätzen mit **was/were**
(Kapitel 10 Themenwortschatz)
ist kein **did/didn't** nötig!

Was the soup hot enough?
No, it wasn't.
War die Suppe heiß genug? Nein.

Die Wortstellung von Adverbien

Häufigkeitsadverbien stehen im Englischen vor dem Vollverb (siehe S. 33). In Sätzen mit dem Hilfsverb **to be** ist die Wortstellung dagegen wie im Deutschen.

The weather in Dublin is often rainy.
Das Wetter in Dublin ist oft regnerisch.

Adverbien des Ortes stehen hinter dem direkten Objekt bzw. dem Verb.

I don't like it here.
Mir gefällt es hier nicht.

Adverbien der Zeit stehen dagegen meist am Satzende, gelegentlich auch am Satzanfang.

I phoned you yesterday.
Ich habe dich gestern angerufen.
Yesterday I was ill.
Gestern war ich krank.

Kommen Adverbien des Ortes und der Zeit in einem Satz vor, dann lautet die Grundregel für die Wortstellung am Satzende: Ort vor Zeit!

I was born there in 1940.
Ich bin 1940 dort geboren worden.

Jahreszahlen

Merken Sie sich zu den Zahlen (siehe Kapitel 2) noch **a/one thousand** (*Tausend*), dann können Sie alle Jahreszahlen bilden.

1984
nineteen eighty-four

1066
ten sixty-six

1558
fifteen fifty-eight

2009
two thousand and nine

2018
twenty eighteen oder **two thousand and eighteen**

4

Lesen Sie die Jahresangaben.

e 1812

f 1940

a 1066

b 1588

g 1968

h 1999

c 1616

d 1789

i 2010

j 2032

5 🦖

Bilden Sie Fragen in der einfachen Vergangenheit. Achten Sie auf die korrekten Verbformen.

a When / be / Sheila / born?
When was Sheila born?
....

b When / move / she / to Islington?
....
....

c Where / be / she / born?
....
....

d Why / not go back / she / to the country?
....
....

6

Setzen Sie die Wortreihen fort.

a dinner, lunch, *breakfast*

b Gran, Dad,

c much, more,

d English, Italian,

e pork, beef,

f nice, attractive,

g wine, juice,

h ourselves, yourselves,

7

Schreiben Sie die Sätze neu und setzen Sie die Adverbien an der richtigen Stelle ein.

a Andy cooks the meals.
(never / on Sundays)
Andy never cooks the meals
on Sundays.

b He checks his e-mails.
(always / in the morning)

c He eats fruit.
(often / from the market)

d Andy does his homework.
(usually / in the evening /
at Lisa's place)

e He tidied up his room.
(yesterday / morning)

8

Reagieren Sie auf diese
Fragen zu Ihrer Biografie.

a I was born in 1980. What about you?

....

....

b My family lived in Glasgow.
What about your family?

....

....

c We had Sunday roast every Sunday.
What about you?

....

....

d My father worked as a waiter.
What about your father?

....

....

e My mother was from Newcastle.
What about your mother?

....

....

9

◉ 094

Hören Sie die Sätze auf der
CD. Geben Sie Kurzantwor-
ten in der einfachen Ver-
gangenheit und stellen Sie
die Aussagen anschließend
richtig. Sie hören zunächst
ein Beispiel.

Zwischentest 2

1 Welche Form des Adjektivs ist richtig? Kreuzen Sie es an.

a Paula is now
- ☐ happy
- ☐ happier
- ☐ happiest

than she was.

b She has got
- ☐ nice
- ☐ nicer
- ☐ nicest

English friends.

c Philip is her
- ☐ good
- ☐ better
- ☐ best

friend in London.

d She is not
- ☐ depressed
- ☐ more depressed
- ☐ most depressed

now.

e But she has still got the
- ☐ uncomfortable
- ☐ more uncomfortable
- ☐ most uncomfortable

room at her B&B.

f Flats in Islington are
- ☐ expensive
- ☐ more expensive
- ☐ most expensive

than they were.

von 6 Punkten

2 Was sagen Sie, wenn …

a … Sie sagen möchten, dass etwas Spaß machen wird?

b … Sie sagen wollen, dass Sie bei den Hausaufgaben helfen können?

c … Sie fragen wollen, was jemand dieses Wochenende vorhat?

d … Sie jemanden bitten möchten, die Musik leiser zu drehen?

e … Sie sagen möchten, dass Sie keine Zeit haben?

f … Sie fragen möchten, wer die langweiligen Hausarbeiten machen wird?

g … Sie fragen wollen, wann jemand geboren wurde?

h … Sie fragen möchten, wie das Essen in Deutschland ist?

von 8 Punkten

3 Welches Wort passt? Kreuzen Sie es an.

a We went to a café and had
☐ any
☐ some
☐ something
coffee.

b We didn't do
☐ any
☐ some
☐ anything
homework yesterday evening.

c We listened to
☐ any
☐ some
☐ something
heavy metal.

d Have you got
☐ any
☐ some
☐ anything
Italian wine?

e We haven't got
☐ something
☐ anything
☐ some
Italian here.

f But we have got
☐ any
☐ some
☐ something
Spanish wines.

von 6 Punkten

4 Hören Sie drei Telefongespräche. Notieren Sie, was die beiden Gesprächspartner wann vorhaben.

◉ 095

a Aktivität / Wochentag, Uhrzeit

....

b Aktivität / Wochentag, Uhrzeit

....

c Aktivität / Wochentag, Uhrzeit

....

von 6 Punkten

5 Lesen Sie die Informationen über London. Sie brauchen nicht jedes Wort zu verstehen! Notieren Sie drei Sehenswürdigkeiten und geben Sie zu jeder eine Zusatzinformation.

The best way to see London is on a boat trip on the River Thames. You can get off and see the Tower of London, where they keep the Crown Jewels. Or you can go and see St Paul's Cathedral. This has a fantastic view of London. The Tate Modern is very popular and gives exhibitions of modern art. Or you can go to the Globe Theatre where there are excellent Shakespeare performances. And last but not least you can go all the way to Greenwich by boat. This is a beautiful place and it's famous for Greenwich Mean Time.

a Sehenswürdigkeit & Zusatzinformation

....

....

b Sehenswürdigkeit & Zusatzinformation

....

....

c Sehenswürdigkeit & Zusatzinformation

....

....

⬭ **von 6 Punkten**

6 Welches Wort passt? Kreuzen Sie es an.

a Andy and Lisa
☐ want
☐ went
☐ when
to the halfpipe yesterday evening.

b After that they
☐ dad
☐ do
☐ did
some homework together.

c Yesterday Sheila and Mahmoud
☐ had
☐ head
☐ hard
some coffee together.

d It
☐ where
☐ was
☐ were
a very pleasant evening.

e Paula and Philip
☐ please
☐ place
☐ played
badminton for an hour and a half.

f On Sunday Philip
☐ cooked
☐ checked
☐ came
beef for lunch.

⬭ **von 6 Punkten**

7 Bilden Sie Sätze mit *going to.*

a What / they / do?

....

b Andy / do / homework.

....

c Lisa / help / with it.

....

d Paula and Philip / play / badminton next week.

....

e Philip / cook / the Sunday roast.

....

f Sheila and Mahmoud / not have / coffee together today.

....

○ **von 6 Punkten**

8 Wie lautet die korrekte Kurzantwort?

a May I have this CD, Dad?

No, ...

b Can't you turn down that music?

Yes, ...

c Can Paula understand her landlady?

No, ...

d Can't Paula find a flat?

No, ...

e Must they hurry to the boat?

Yes, ...

f Must we see everything in one day?

No, ...

○ **von 6 Punkten**

Sie haben

○

Punkte von 50 erreicht.

BEWERTUNG

45–50
★★★★
Very good
Kompliment! Ihre Mühe hat sich wirklich gelohnt.

35–44
★★★ **Good**
Prima — Sie haben sehr viel gelernt!

25–34
★★ OK
Vieles klappt schon ziemlich gut, aber üben Sie weiter an den Stellen, die Ihnen noch Schwierigkeiten bereiten.

Weniger als 25
★ **You can do better**
Sie sind schon sehr weit gekommen, aber es lohnt sich bestimmt, jetzt nochmals die Kapitel zu wiederholen, die Sie noch nicht so gut können.

12

EINE REISE PLANEN

In diesem Kapitel lernen Sie

Wünsche und Meinungen zu äußern →

Vorhersagen für die Zukunft zu treffen →

Vorschläge und Gegenvorschläge zu machen →

Wortschatz zum Dialog

◎ 096

business trip
Geschäftsreise

United States
Vereinigte Staaten

to **hope**
hoffen

to **give**
geben

conference
Konferenz

to **last**
dauern

free
frei

near
nahe, in der Nähe von

business
Geschäft, Business

to **come off**
gelingen, klappen;
hier: zustande kommen

will
werden (Futur)

go-ahead
Zustimmung;
hier: grünes Licht

by
hier: spätestens bis

You've got it now.
Jetzt hast du's.

A great idea!

◎ 097

Paula and Philip are planning a business trip to the United States.

 **PAULA:** This is a great idea. I hope that the trip really comes off.

 PHILIP: Well, Mr Butler wants us to plan it and he will give us the go-ahead by the end of the week.

 OK. He says the trip will be in September. The conference is in New Brunswick, New Jersey, and will last two days. And then we have a day free to go and see the sights in New York City.

 Well, let's look at New Brunswick on the Internet first.

 No, Philip, that's New Brunswick in Canada. We want New Brunswick near New York. You've got it now. That's it.

— **Paula and Philip are going to Canada ☐ to the USA ☐ .**
— **The conference will last two days ☐ three days ☐ .**

◉ 099

PHILIP: Well, here are the hotels. We'll have a look at the prices and where they are later. The conference centre is here. It's all close together.

PAULA: And we have to look at the flights from London to New York. Let's look at the sights in Manhattan. It will be the first time for both of us!

What would you like to see there? The Empire State Building?

Yes, of course. And Central Park. And the Statue of Liberty and Ellis Island. But I don't really know what else. Shall we find a good website?

But, Paula, shouldn't we get at least some information together today for Mr Butler so he can decide about the trip? And then InterChip USA must confirm the trip. Couldn't we do that now?

Yes, I think we could have it all ready this afternoon.

— It's the first time in New York
  ☐ for Paula ☐ for both of them.
— Paula wants to see the Empire State Building. ☐ right ☐ wrong

Wortschatz zum Dialog

◎ 098

hotel
Hotel

to **have a look at …**
einen Blick auf … werfen

later
später

centre
Zentrum

close
nahe

flight
Flug

both
beide

ready
fertig, bereit

to **have to**
müssen

so
hier: damit, sodass

shall
soll(en)

to **confirm**
bestätigen

website
Website

information
Information(en)

Fragewörter

◉ 100

1 Setzen Sie das richtige Fragewort ein.

a _How_ (Wie) old are you?

b .... (Wo) do you work?

c .... (Wer) knows your birthday?

d .... (Wann) did you start learning English?

e .... (Was) did you have for dinner last night?

f .... (Wie viel) do you earn*?

* to earn — _verdienen_

2 Beantworten Sie die Fragen.

a Where do you live?
I live in Potsdam, near Berlin.

b Do you have coffee or tea for breakfast?
....
....

c When did you go to bed last night?
....

d How much coffee do you drink per day?
....
....

e Why do you want to learn English?
....
....

3 Wie heißt das auf Englisch?

a _to give_
geben

b ....
in der Nähe von

c ....
frei

d ....
später

e ....
Flug

f ....
fertig, bereit

g ....
Zentrum

h ....
Geschäftsreise

i ....
hoffen

j ....
dauern

Die Zukunft mit *will*

Vorhersagen über die Zukunft bildet man mit **will** *(werden)* und der Grundform des Verbs. Die Verneinung lautet **won't** (**will not**), die Kurzform **'ll**.

In the future we robots will do the dishes.
In der Zukunft werden wir Roboter den Abwasch machen.

And we won't complain.
Und wir werden uns nicht beschweren.

Mit **will** drücken Sie neben Vorhersagen für die Zukunft auch spontane Entschlüsse und Angebote aus:

We'll have a coffee later.
Wir werden nachher Kaffee trinken.

Um eine <mark>Frage</mark> zu stellen, drehen Sie Subjekt und Verb einfach um.

Wirst du beim Umzug mitmachen?

Für <mark>Kurzantworten</mark> rückt will nach hinten.

Ja, werde ich.

Nein, werde ich nicht.

Won't they come with us?
Werden sie nicht mit uns kommen?

Yes, they will.
Doch, das werden sie.

No, they won't.
Nein, das werden sie nicht.

Die Hilfsverben *could, would* und *should*

Mit could und would können Sie eine höfliche Frage oder eine Bitte formulieren.
Mit shouldn't I/we ...? leiten Sie einen höflichen Vorschlag ein.

Could you repeat that?
Könntest du das wiederholen?

Of course. Would you marry me?
Natürlich. Würdest du mich heiraten?

Shouldn't we ask your mother first?
Sollten wir nicht zuerst deine Mutter fragen?

Vom Verb zum Substantiv

Mit der Endung -er können Sie – genau wie im Deutschen – von vielen Verben Substantive ableiten:

to **teach** *unterrichten, lehren*

teacher *Lehrer(in)*

to **work** *arbeiten*	**work**er *Arbeiter(in)*
to **play** *spielen*	**play**er *Spieler(in)*
to **drive** *fahren*	**driv**er *Fahrer(in)*
to **speak** *sprechen*	**speak**er *Sprecher(in)*
to **listen** *zuhören*	**listen**er *Zuhörer(in)*
to **read** *lesen*	**read**er *Leser(in)*
to **write** *schreiben*	**writ**er *Schriftsteller(in)*

4

Lesen Sie die Infos über
New York und ergänzen
Sie die passenden Wörter.

New York City is one of the most famous
(a) *cities* .... in the world and the
biggest city in the (b) .... It is
best to see it on a business (c) .... ! You
don't pay for the flight and the hotel, but
you can see all the famous sights. What (d) ....
you like to see there? The Empire State (e) .... is on
(f) .... Avenue. For a long time it was the biggest
building in the (g) .... Take a walk around
(h) .... Park. And go and see the Statue of Liberty
and Ellis Island. But I don't really know what else. Find out more
at our (i) ....

5

Ergänzen Sie *will* oder *won't*.

a The trip will be in August. —
No, it *won't* ....
It *will* .... be in September.

b The conference will last four days. —
No, it ....
It .... last two days.

c The hotels will be cheap. —
No, they ....
They .... be expensive.

d New York will be boring. —
No, it ....
It .... be fantastic.

6

◎ 101

Hören Sie den Dialog und kreuzen Sie an, welche Aussage richtig und welche falsch ist.

a They are going to Paris in the USA.
☐ right ☐ wrong

b The trip will be in June.
☐ right ☐ wrong

c Hazel wants to see the most famous sights.
☐ right ☐ wrong

d Kevin wants to get some information together.
☐ right ☐ wrong

7

Welches Wort passt hier? Ergänzen Sie es und reagieren Sie mit den Vorgaben in Klammern oder Ihren eigenen Ideen.

 would
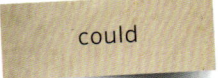 could
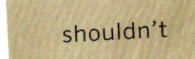 shouldn't
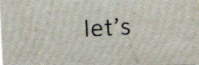 let's
 shall

a *Shall* .... we go for a walk in the park? — Yes, ... (good idea).

b .... you like to have some coffee? — Yes, ...
.... (café over there).

c .... you help me with this maths? — Yes, of course ....
....

d .... do the shopping now.
— No, ... (later).

e .... we buy some fruit? —
Yes, ... (great idea).

8

Setzen Sie die Sätze ins Futur entweder mit will (+) oder won't (–).

a Chris called the office this afternoon. (+)

Chris will call the office
this afternoon.

b James cooked the potatoes. (–)

....
....

c They confirmed the trip. (–)

....
....

d We invited all our friends. (+)

....
....

e I had some wine. (+)

....
....

f You stayed a bit longer. (–)

....
....

g They ate in an expensive restaurant. (+)

....
....

9

 102

Hören Sie die Wörter auf der CD und sprechen Sie sie nach. Achten Sie auf die unterschiedliche Aussprache des „a".

already	same
uncomfortable	cathedral
village	parents
walk	lamb
bar	about
takeaway	apple
want	attic
fantastic	landlady
altogether	market
awful	woman

13

VERKEHRS-MITTEL

In diesem Kapitel lernen Sie

Reiseauskünfte einzuholen →

Fahrkarten zu kaufen →

Uhrzeiten zu verstehen und anzugeben →

Wortschatz zum Dialog

◉ 103

luggage
Gepäck

train
Zug

suitcase
Koffer

to leave
verlassen; abreisen

plane
Flugzeug

on the way
unterwegs

way
Weg

heavy
schwer; stark
(z. B. Verkehr, Regen)

only
nur

to change
wechseln;
hier: umsteigen

once
einmal

till (= until)
bis

to get (to)
hinkommen, ankommen

taxi
Taxi

announcement
Durchsage,
Ankündigung

announcer
Ansager(in)

passenger
Passagier(in)

station
Station, Bahnhof

immediately
sofort, umgehend

security
Sicherheit

reason
Grund

bomb alarm
Bombenalarm

outside
draußen,
nach draußen

as ... as
so ... wie

quickly
schnell

possible
möglich

already
schon

late
hier: zu spät

past
hier: nach (zeitlich)

On the way to Heathrow

◎ 104

PHILIP: Here we are. We can get our tickets here.

PAULA: This luggage is very heavy.

We only have to change once and then we can just sit on the train till we get to Heathrow.

Wouldn't it be better to take a taxi?

Uff, these suitcases really are heavy! What's that announcement?

ANNOUNCER: Will all passengers please leave the station immediately for security reasons.

Oh no! That sounds like a bomb alarm again. Come on. We have to get outside as quickly as possible.

Here we are. We're already late. It's 12:47 now. And our plane is at ten minutes past three.

— They want to take ☐ the train ☐ a taxi to Heathrow.
— There is ☐ a technical problem ☐ an alarm at the station.

◎ 106

 **PHILIP:** If we take a taxi, we should be there in time. Look there's one over there.

 PAULA: But if the traffic is heavy, we'll miss the plane.

 (to taxi driver) Heathrow Airport, Terminal 5, please. As fast as you can.

 DRIVER: With this traffic, you can see for yourself how fast we can go, mate!

 ANNOUNCER: *(at Heathrow Airport)* Last call for Ms Paula Schneider and Mr Philip Elton. Please go to your check-in desk immediately.

 That's us. We have to check in over there. The check-in clerks are still there. Come on. Let's run.

 The 15:10 flight to New York?

 CLERK: Yes, you're OK, but you haven't got much time. If you hurry, you'll catch your plane.

— **Paula and Philip have to take**
  ☐ a taxi
  ☐ a bus to Heathrow.
— **There are**
  ☐ announcers
  ☐ clerks at the check-in desk.

Wortschatz zum Dialog

◎ 105

traffic
Verkehr

to **miss**
verpassen

driver
Fahrer(in)

airport
Flughafen

fast
schnell

to **check in**
einchecken

to **run**
rennen, laufen

bus
Bus

if
wenn

in time
rechtzeitig

mate
Mann, Kumpel

call
(An)Ruf; hier: Aufruf

check-in desk
Check-in-Schalter

clerk
Angestellte(r)

to **catch**
fangen, hier: erreichen

Uhrzeit

1 Schreiben Sie die Uhrzeiten auf jeweils zwei Arten auf.

a 9:15

It's *(a) quarter past nine / nine fifteen.*

b 11:30

It's ....

c 8:16

It's ....

d 3:50

It's ....

2 In jedem Satz stecken ein bis zwei Fehler. Korrigieren Sie.

a ~~How's~~ What's the time?

b It 12:30 — twelve thirty o'clock.

c It's close to middlenight.

d It's five watch.

e It's 9:30 — half ten.

f It's 20 behind 2 o'clock.

g It's 6:45 — three quarter seven.

3 Wie heißt das auf Englisch?

a *bus*
Bus

b
verpassen

c
schnell

d
Koffer

e
Flugzeug

f
Fahrer

g
Verkehr

h
verlassen

i
Zug

j
rennen

Der Bedingungssatz

Ein Bedingungssatz besteht immer aus einer Bedingung und einer Folge. Im Englischen formulieren Sie Bedingungen mit dem Wörtchen **if** *(wenn, falls).*

Die Zeitenfolge ist in Bedingungssätzen genau festgelegt. Wenn Sie von Bedingungen sprechen, die <mark>wahrscheinlich</mark> sind, verwenden Sie im **if**-Satz die einfache Gegenwart und im Folgesatz **will/won't**.

Achtung: Im **if**-Satz steht <mark>nie</mark> **will/won't**!

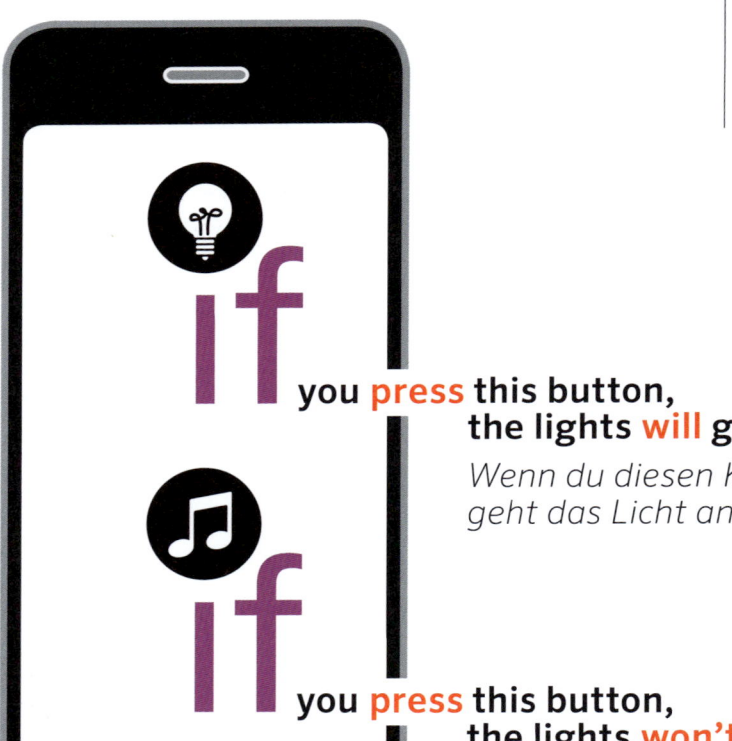

if you **press** this button,
the lights **will** go on.
Wenn du diesen Knopf drückst, geht das Licht an.

if you **press** this button,
the lights **won't** go on,
but you**'ll** hear some music.
Wenn du diesen Knopf drückst, geht nicht das Licht an, sondern du hörst Musik.

Die beiden Satzhälften von Bedingungssätzen können umgedreht werden. Im Englischen steht dann kein Komma vor if.

You'll get a pizza if you press this button.

Du bekommst eine Pizza, wenn du diesen Knopf drückst.

Statt will kann im Folgesatz auch ein Hilfsverb wie could, would oder should stehen:

if you press this button now, your dress should be here tomorrow.

Wenn du jetzt diesen Knopf drückst, sollte dein Kleid morgen hier sein.

Die Verwendung von *have to*

Sätze mit dem Hilfsverb **must** *(müssen)* klingen im Englischen häufig zu abrupt, fast schon unhöflich. Sie können stattdessen **have to** verwenden.

Es drückt aus, dass etwas dringend erforderlich ist oder von jemandem angeordnet wurde.

Sparky has to wait outside.
Sparky muss draußen warten.

Die Verneinung **don't/doesn't have to** bedeutet ebenso wie im Deutschen *nicht müssen*, während **must not** *nicht dürfen* heißt (siehe S. 107).

4

Wählen Sie ein passendes Verb und ergänzen Sie es zusammen mit *have to*. Es kann mehrere Möglichkeiten geben.

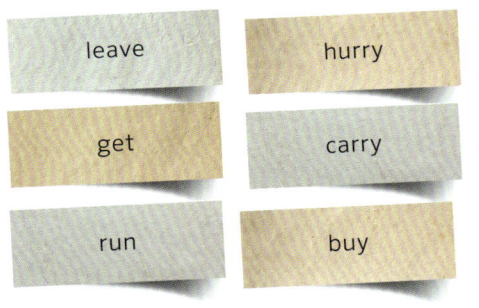

leave hurry

get carry

run buy

a Paula and Philip *have to buy/get* their tickets to Heathrow at the Underground station.

b Paula .... her suitcases herself.

c The passengers .... the station immediately.

d At Heathrow they .... to the check-in desk.

e Both .... to the plane.

5 📱

In diesen Bedingungssätzen fehlen entweder der *if*-Satz oder der Folgesatz. Vollenden Sie die Sätze mit eigenen Beispielen.

a If James is here in time, *we'll take him with us.*

b *If* ....
.... I will be home at seven.

c If Paula goes to London, ...
....
....

d If Steve and Billy don't run, ...
....
....

e *If* ....
....
.... he will catch his plane.

f If we invite Jess, ...
....
....

Flight	Time	Destination	Gate
↑ **Departures**			✈
VX 161	06:45	LONDON	A17
AQ 326	06:55	NEW YORK	B3
TG 348	07:10	PARIS	C15
NK4587	07:25	TOKYO	A9
MX6261	07:30	BANGKOK	D19
AA 783	07:45	ROME	B8
OX9023	08:10	MUNICH	C2
AN 845	08:30	AMSTERDAM	D5

6

Oben sind die nächsten *departures* (Abflüge) zu verschiedenen *destinations* (Zielen) angezeigt. Kreuzen Sie an, was zutrifft.

---

a When is the next flight to New York?
- ☐ five to seven
- ☐ five past six
- ☐ quarter to seven

b When is the next flight to Tokyo?
- ☐ half past eight
- ☐ seven twenty-five
- ☐ twenty-five minutes to seven

c When is the next flight to Amsterdam?
- ☐ half past nine
- ☐ nine thirty
- ☐ half past eight

d When is the next flight to Rome?
- ☐ quarter past seven
- ☐ seven forty-five
- ☐ quarter to seven

e When is the next flight to London?
- ☐ six fifty-five
- ☐ quarter past six
- ☐ quarter to seven

7

⊚ 108

Hören Sie die CD und notieren Sie, wie viele Fahrkarten für welches Verkehrsmittel gekauft werden. Tragen Sie auch das Reiseziel und den Preis in die Tabelle ein.

1 Wie viele? *4 tickets*

Wofür? ....

Wohin? ....

Wie teuer? ....

2 Wie viele? ....

Wofür? ....

Wohin? ....

Wie teuer? ....

3 Wie viele? ....

Wofür? ....

Wohin? ....

Wie teuer? ....

4 Wie viele? ....

Wofür? ....

Wohin? ....

Wie teuer? ....

8

Paul und Emily widersprechen sich ständig. Was auch immer Paul sagt, Emily behauptet das Gegenteil. Übernehmen Sie die Rolle von Emily.

a Paul: These oranges are cheap.

Emily: *No, they're not.*
They're expensive!

b Paul: The music is very quiet.

Emily: ....

....

c Paul: That woman is so young.

Emily: ....

....

d Paul: The film was fantastic.

Emily: ....

....

e Paul: The airport is really big.

Emily: ....

....

f Paul: That man looks happy.

Emily: ....

....

14

NACH DEM WEG FRAGEN

**In diesem Kapitel
lernen Sie**

nach dem Weg
zu fragen →

den Weg zu
beschreiben →

das Verständnis
zu bestätigen →

Wortschatz zum Dialog

◉ 109

arrival
Ankunft

to **wear**
(Kleidung) tragen

uniform
Uniform

counter
Schalter

on the right
rechts

car
Auto

shuttle
Pendelbus (bzw. -zug)

strong
kräftig, stark

the one who ...
derjenige, der ...

to **pick up**
abholen

excuse me
Entschuldigung

to **run**
hier: fahren, verkehren

car rental
Autovermietung

clear
klar, verständlich

down
hinunter, (nach) unten

accent
Akzent

Arrival in New York

◎ 110

Philip and Paula are at Terminal 7 of John F. Kennedy International Airport.

PAULA: Where do we go? Let's ask that man, the one who is wearing the red uniform. Excuse me, where are the car rentals here?

MAN: Well, go down that way and the car rental counters are on the right. If you want to pick up your car, you have to take the shuttle that runs from AirTrain Station C.

Yes, that's all clear. Thank you very much.

PHILIP: Hey, Paula, I didn't understand half of what he said.

Well, I understood everything.

But he had a very strong accent.

Anyway, let's do what he said.

— Paula and Philip are at the airport in ☐ New Brunswick ☐ New York.
— They get information from a man ☐ in a red uniform ☐ in a red car.

◉ 112

PAULA: Hello, we'd like to pick up this rental car that our company reserved for us. Here's the voucher. Can you confirm that everything is OK, and tell us where we have to go?

CLERK: Yes, of course, Ms Schneider. Sign here, please. Can I see your driver's license? Thank you. Now you have to take the shuttle and go to the Van Wyck Expressway, which is where the rental offices are. You can pick up the keys there. Have a safe trip, and have fun in the States.

Thank you very much.

PHILIP: (later) I think you should drive, Paula. You're used to driving on the right. I'll navigate.

Philip, there's no need for that. All the cars have a navigation system!

— All cars have a ☐ voucher system ☐ navigation system.
— They can pick up the keys ☐ at the rental office ☐ at the rental counter.

Wortschatz zum Dialog

◉ 111

company
Firma

to **tell**
mitteilen, erzählen

to **sign**
unterschreiben

driver's license
Führerschein

key
Schlüssel

safe
sicher

to **drive**
fahren

navigation system
Navigationssystem

rental car
Mietwagen

to **reserve**
reservieren

voucher
Gutschein; hier: Reservierungsbestätigung

which
welche(r, s);
der/die/das

to **be used to**
gewöhnt sein an

to **navigate**
navigieren, führen

need
Notwendigkeit

Orts - und Richtungs- angaben

◎ 113

Drive straight on and you will come to a roundabout.
Fahren Sie immer gerade- aus, dann kommen Sie zu einem Kreisverkehr.

Turn right at the first road you come to.
Biegen Sie an der ersten Straße rechts ab.

Take the third turning on the left.
Nehmen Sie die dritte Querstraße rechts.

Turn right at the second traffic lights.
Biegen Sie an der zweiten Ampel rechts ab.

Go straight on to the crossroads.
Gehen Sie gerade- aus bis zur Kreuzung.

Park here!
Parken Sie hier!

Then it's only two minutes' walk.
Dann sind es nur noch zwei Minuten zu Fuß.

1 Schreiben Sie das passende Wort in die Lücke.

How do I (a) *get* to the police station? Well, (b) .... straight on to the second traffic lights. Then (c) .... left into Park Street and (d) .... the first turning on the right. After a hundred metres you'll see the police station on your (e) .... Don't (f) .... in front of it. There is a car park (g) .... the house, just turn left into the courtyard.

2 Welche Angaben drücken dasselbe aus?

a Go straight on to the traffic lights.

b Turn left at the third crossroads.

c Take the second turning on your right.

d Turn left at the roundabout.

1 *Biegen Sie am Kreisverkehr links ab.*

2 *Nehmen Sie die zweite Querstraße zu Ihrer Rechten.*

3 *Biegen Sie an der dritten Kreuzung links ab.*

4 *Fahren Sie geradeaus bis zur Ampel.*

3 Wie heißt das auf Englisch?

a *to drive*
fahren

b
stark

c
Auto

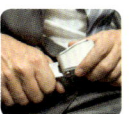

d
sicher

e
Führerschein

f
Schlüssel

g
unterschreiben

h
Firma

i
rechts

j
erzählen

Relativsätze

Personen oder Sachen können mit Relativsätzen <mark>näher bestimmt</mark> werden. Ein Relativsatz wird durch ein Relativpronomen eingeleitet, zum Beispiel durch **who** bzw. **which/that** *(der/die/das)*.

The girl who is allergic to the sun still goes to the beach.

Das Mädchen, das auf Sonne allergisch ist, geht immer noch zum Strand.

Die Wahl des richtigen Relativpronomens hängt vom Bezugswort ab:

Bei <mark>Personen</mark> verwenden Sie **who**, bei <mark>Sachen</mark> **which** oder **that**.

Manchmal wird das Relativpronomen **that** auch bei Personen verwendet, allerdings ist **who** in diesem Fall gebräuchlicher.

Im Englischen werden Relativsätze meist <mark>nicht durch Kommas abgetrennt</mark>.

A tree which/that loses its needles has to be watered.

Ein Baum, der seine Nadeln verliert, muss gewässert werden.

My car is parked in the market square, which is in front of the church.

Mein Auto parkt auf dem Marktplatz, der vor der Kirche liegt.

Nur Relativsätze, die zusätzliche, nicht unbedingt notwendige Informationen enthalten, werden durch ein Komma abgetrennt. Diese Sätze werden mit dem Relativpronomen **which** bzw. **who** eingeleitet, niemals mit **that**.

Eine Besonderheit sind im Englischen die Relativsätze ohne Relativpronomen. Das ==Relativpronomen== kann immer dann ==weggelassen werden==, wenn das Bezugswort Objekt im Satz ist. Das wird Ihnen in der gesprochenen Sprache häufig begegnen.

The first butterfly I saw already sat on my knee.

Der erste Schmetterling, den ich sah, saß schon auf meinem Knie.

==Tipp:== Wenn Sie immer ein Relativpronomen verwenden, machen Sie keinen Fehler!

4

Ergänzen Sie *who* oder *which/that*. Manchmal ist kein Relativpronomen nötig.

a New Brunswick is a city *which/* *that* .... is near New York.

b There is also a New Brunswick .... is in Canada.

c It is Paula .... wants to see the sights of Manhattan.

d Paula wants to see everything .... is in the museum on Ellis Island.

e They must get together the information .... Mr Butler needs.

f Paula will answer any question .... Mr Butler has.

5

Diese Relativsätze sind durcheinandergeraten. Bringen Sie die Elemente in die richtige Reihenfolge.

a at the cinema / Philip / Sheila called / who was.
Sheila called Philip, who was *at the cinema.*
....

b has to / Andy / reserved / pick up / that he / the car.
....
....
....
....

c drank immediately / bought a coffee / which he / Stewart.
....
....
....
....

d Jo / in America / to Martin / an e-mail / who is / is writing.
....
....
....
....

e am taking / to the airport / the train / I / that goes.
....
....
....
....

6

Lesen Sie die E-Mail. Sie kennen nicht alle Wörter, aber Sie werden alles verstehen. Korrigieren Sie danach die falschen Aussagen mündlich.

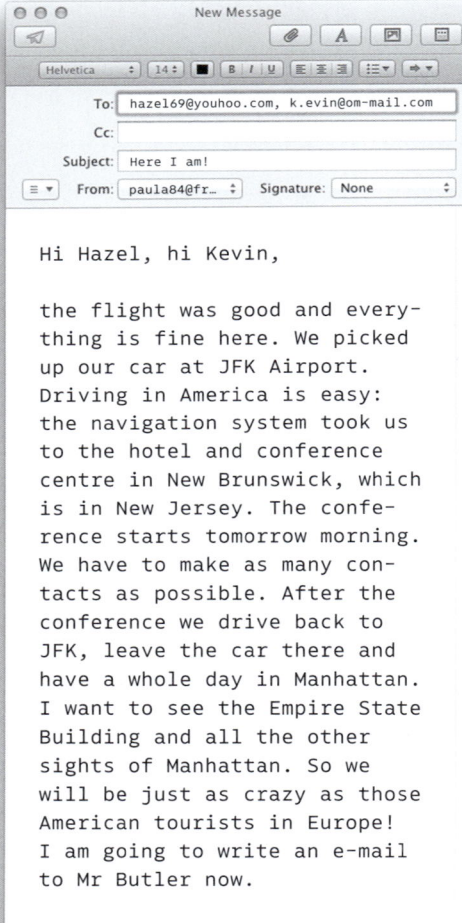

New Message

To: hazel69@youhoo.com, k.evin@om-mail.com
Cc:
Subject: Here I am!
From: paula84@fr...   Signature: None

Hi Hazel, hi Kevin,

the flight was good and everything is fine here. We picked
up our car at JFK Airport.
Driving in America is easy:
the navigation system took us
to the hotel and conference
centre in New Brunswick, which
is in New Jersey. The conference starts tomorrow morning.
We have to make as many con-
tacts as possible. After the
conference we drive back to
JFK, leave the car there and
have a whole day in Manhattan.
I want to see the Empire State
Building and all the other
sights of Manhattan. So we
will be just as crazy as those
American tourists in Europe!
I am going to write an e-mail
to Mr Butler now.

Best wishes, Paula

a They picked up their car in New Brunswick.

b The conference centre is in Canada.

c After the conference they will take the train to Manhattan.

d They have two days for the sights in Manhattan.

e Mr Butler is going to write an e-mail to Paula.

7

(◎) 114

Sie werden nach dem Weg gefragt. Hören Sie die CD und verwenden Sie diese Vorgaben für Ihre Weg-beschreibung.

1 links an erster Ampel
Turn left at the first traffic lights.

2 rechts an nächster Kreuzung

3 erste Abzweigung links, dann eine Gehminute

4 geradeaus, Bahnhof links

5 richtiger Weg, wenn Restaurant rechts

6 zweite Ausfahrt, dann geradeaus, bis links das Konferenzzentrum ist

*exit – *Ausfahrt, Ausgang*

8

Machen Sie aus zwei Sätzen einen. Verwenden Sie dabei einen Relativsatz.

a A taxi took us to the station.

It was very expensive.
The taxi which/that took us
to the station was very expensive.

b A man gave them the keys.

He was really old.
The man

c I was at a concert last week.

It was fantastic.
The concert

d A shuttle goes to the expressway.

It was late.
The shuttle

e A woman came to the office.

She is our new colleague.
The woman

f I bought a small coffee. It was cold.
The small coffee

15

IM HOTEL

**In diesem Kapitel
lernen Sie**

Vor- und Nachteile
eines Hotels zu
beschreiben →

mitzuteilen, was
Sie alles erledigt
haben →

jemanden um
Auskunft zu bitten →

Wortschatz zum Dialog

◉ 115

to arrive
ankommen

foyer
Eingangshalle, Foyer

to unpack
auspacken

shower
Dusche

hot
heiß

light
Licht

reception
Empfang, Rezeption

to repair
reparieren

just
gerade, eben

been
gewesen

impression
Eindruck

America
Amerika

never ... before
noch nie

main
Haupt-

to work
hier: funktionieren

next
nächste(r, s)

yet
schon

personally
persönlich

probably
wahrscheinlich

Just arrived!

◉ 116

Paula and Philip have arrived at their hotel in New Brunswick. They have checked in and been to their rooms. Now they are in the foyer and are talking about their first impressions of America.

PHILIP: I've unpacked and I've just had a shower. The shower is great. Lots and lots of hot water, not like some hotels I know in England.

PAULA: Yes, I've had a shower, too. I've never stayed at a hotel like this before.

But the main light in my room doesn't work.

Have you called reception?

Yes, someone is going to repair it in the next 20 minutes.

Have you met any of the people from the conference yet?

No, I haven't. I don't know any of them personally. We'll probably meet some of them this evening or at breakfast tomorrow morning.

— Paula and Philip are talking
☐ in the foyer ☐ in Philip's room.
— The main light in Paula's room doesn't work. ☐ right ☐ wrong

◉ 118

PAULA: Have you found out where the breakfast room is?

PHILIP: No, I haven't yet. But it's not down here. It's probably on the first floor — the Americans call it the second floor! I'm looking forward to a real American breakfast: eggs "sunny side up", hash browns and bagels.

Oh, yes, breakfast is at seven o'clock and the conference begins at nine.

And have you looked through all the materials once again?

Yes, I've checked everything.

Shall we go for a walk and get a first impression of the conference centre?

Yes, let's do that.

— Philip is looking forward to a real English breakfast.
☐ right ☐ wrong
— Paula has looked through the materials for the conference.
☐ right ☐ wrong

Wortschatz zum Dialog

◉ 117

floor
Fußboden; hier: Etage

American
Amerikaner(in)

American
amerikanisch

egg
Ei

egg "sunny side up"
Spiegelei

hash browns
Kartoffelpuffer, Rösti

bagel
Bagel
(Gebäck aus Brotteig)

to begin
beginnen

to **find out**
herausfinden

not ... yet
noch nicht

to **look forward to**
sich freuen auf

sunny
sonnig

side
Seite

to **look through**
durchsehen

through
durch

material
Material

once again
noch einmal

Im Hotel

◉ 119

mirror
Spiegel

TV (television)
Fernseher

wardrobe
Kleiderschrank

bed
Bett

chair
Stuhl

desk
Schreibtisch

remote control
Fern-bedienung

light
Licht

tap
Wasserhahn

toilet
Toilette

sink
Waschbecken

bathtub
Badewanne

hairdryer
Föhn

fridge (refrigerator)
Kühlschrank

1 Fügen Sie die passenden Begriffe ein.

The hotel was terrible. I wanted to

(a) *unpack* my suitcase, but couldn't

find a (b) .... for

my clothes*. Then there was no warm

(c) .... in the shower and

no (d) .... to dry

my hair with. When I took the

(e) .... to watch

(f) .... , the lights went off. I tried

to call (g) .... but

nobody answered.

*clothes — *Kleider*

2 Übersetzen Sie die Begriffe, und Sie erfahren, was „Kopfkissen" auf Englisch heißt.

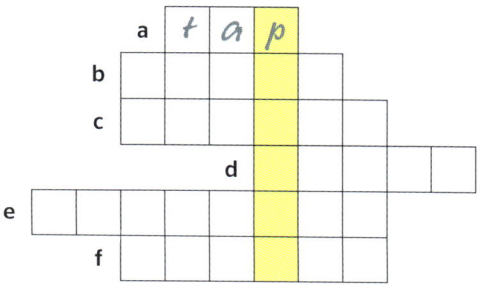

a *Wasserhahn* **d** *Licht*

b *Stuhl* **e** *Kleiderschrank*

c *Toilette* **f** *Dusche*

3 Wie heißt das auf Englisch?

a *light*
Licht

b
reparieren

c
amerikanisch

d
Ei

e
beginnen

f
heiß

g
Etage

h
Rezeption

i
ankommen

j
Dusche

Das *present perfect*

Das *present perfect* wird verwendet, wenn eine Handlung in der Vergangenheit begonnen hat und bis in die Gegenwart andauert oder sie noch beeinflusst. Es baut sozusagen eine Brücke von der Vergangenheit in die Gegenwart.

VERGANGENHEIT

GEGENWART

We**'ve been** on this bus for two hours…
Wir sind seit zwei Stunden in diesem Bus …

…and still don't know where we are going.
… und wissen immer noch nicht, wohin wir fahren.

Das *present perfect* setzt sich zusammen aus dem Hilfsverb to have und dem <mark>Partizip Perfekt</mark> des Vollverbs.

Das Partizip stimmt bei regelmäßigen Verben mit der einfachen Vergangenheit des Verbs (*simple past*, siehe Kapitel 10) überein und hat die Endung **-ed**. In der Regel werden die Kurzformen von **has/have** (**'s/'ve**) verwendet.

I have boarded the bus to Islington.

Ich bin in den Bus nach Islington eingestiegen.

HILFSVERB   PARTIZIP PERFEKT

<mark>Unregelmäßige Verben</mark> haben dagegen meist eigene Formen des Partizips, die auswendig gelernt werden müssen.

She hasn't caught the bus.

Sie hat den Bus nicht erwischt.

GRUND-FORM	SIMPLE PAST	PARTIZIP PERFEKT
do	did	done
be	was/were	been
go	went	gone
get	got	got
have	had	had
write	wrote	written
catch	caught	caught

Eine ausführliche Liste unregelmäßiger Verbformen finden Sie auf S. 287.

Fragen im *present perfect* bilden Sie wieder durch Umstellung von Hilfsverb und Subjekt.

Hat sie beim Umzug mit- gemacht?

In der Kurzantwort wird das Hilfsverb wiederholt.

Ja, hat sie.

Nein, hat sie nicht.

4

Ergänzen Sie die Verben im *present perfect*.

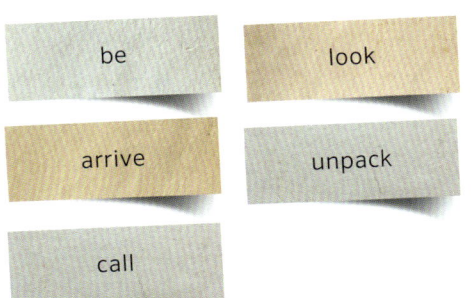

be   look

arrive   unpack

call

a Paula and Philip *have arrived* at their hotel in New Brunswick.

b They .... to their rooms.

c They .... their suitcases.

d Philip .... reception about his light.

e Paula .... through all the materials once again.

5

◉ 120

Hören Sie das Telefongespräch zwischen Philip und Andy und korrigieren Sie die Aussagen.

a Philip is phoning after the first day of the conference.
Philip is phoning after the first morning of the conference.

b He had a real English breakfast.
....

c Paula doesn't understand the Americans.
....
....

d She is having a good time in Manhattan.
....
....

e There are shops in the conference centre with skateboards.
....
....

6

Vervollständigen Sie die folgenden Sätze mit dem Verb und der jeweiligen Zeitform in der Klammer dahinter und lesen Sie sie laut vor.

a Sheila *played* badminton every weekend. (to play; *simple past*)

b I .... a lot of driving in my new job. (to do; Zukunft mit *will*)

c Philip and Paula .... in New York. (to arrive; *present perfect*)

d Mr Jones .... a teacher at our school. (to be; *simple past*)

e Kevin .... some coffee. (to drink; *present progressive*)

f I .... at the cinema. (to be; *present perfect*)

g We .... fish and chips on Friday. (to have; Zukunft mit *going to*)

h Joe .... his suitcase. (to unpack; *present progressive*)

7

Stellen Sie Fragen zu diesen Aussagen im *present perfect*.

a She's been to America before.
Has she been to America before?

b Paula's gone to the airport.

....

....

c We've reserved a rental car in New York.

....

....

d I've already had some tea.

....

....

e She's repaired the hairdryer for me.

....

....

f I've picked up the boss from the airport.

....

....

g They've played tennis before.

....

....

8

Beschreiben Sie in 3 Sätzen, was Sie heute gemacht haben, und in 3 weiteren, was Sie nicht gemacht haben. Wählen Sie dazu aus den vorgegebenen Stichwörtern die passenden aus oder ergänzen Sie andere Aktivitäten.

have some coffee

phone a friend

pack my suitcase

miss the bus

listen to some music

check my e-mails

do some shopping

be happy

I've done this: *I've had some coffee,*

....

....

....

I haven't done this: ....

....

....

....

9

Beantworten Sie die Fragen mit einer Kurzantwort.

a Have you ever met and talked to any Americans?
Yes, I have. /
No, I haven't.

b Have you ever worked with Americans?
....
....

c Have you ever phoned America?
....
....

d Have you ever stayed at an American hotel?
....
....

16
EIN NOTFALL

**In diesem Kapitel
lernen Sie**

Körperteile zu
benennen →

körperliche
Beschwerden
zu beschreiben →

ein Gespräch
mit einem Arzt
zu führen →

Wortschatz zum Dialog

◎ 121

to **shop**
einkaufen

to **knock (down)**
umstoßen

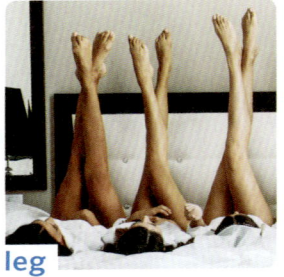

leg
Bein

arm
Arm

to **skate**
hier: Skateboard fahren

left
links

suddenly
plötzlich

pavement
Bürgersteig

doctor
Doktor, Arzt/Ärztin

to **hurt**
hier: wehtun

to **be sorry**
leidtun

to **move**
bewegen

along
entlang

An accident

⊚ 122

Back in Islington: Paula was shopping in Upper Street with Sheila when something or someone knocked Paula down from behind.

 PAULA: Oh, Sheila! My leg! It hurts really awfully. Oh, and my arm, too.

 SKATEBOARDER: I'm terribly sorry. I wasn't skating very fast. And you moved to the left suddenly.

 SHEILA: You were going much too fast. And you shouldn't be on the pavement anyway.

 Shall I call a doctor?

 DOCTOR: No need for that. I'm a doctor. Can I help you?

 If you could, please, doctor. We were just walking along the street when this young man here knocked Paula down on his skateboard.

— Paula and Sheila were shopping in Islington.
  ☐ right ☐ wrong
— ☐ A car ☐ A young man knocked Paula down.

⊚ 124

DOCTOR: Just stay where you are. Don't move. Where does it hurt?

PAULA: The skateboard hit my leg. It's very painful. And I fell on my hand and my wrist and that hurts, too.

Would you like me to call you an ambulance?

No, I don't think that's necessary. If I walk very slowly, I'll be OK.

Well, if it's still painful tomorrow, go and see your doctor.

Thank you very much. It's all right.

SHEILA: And you, young man, you should be much more careful in future. You're lucky your skateboard didn't break her leg. Come on, Paula. Take my arm and walk very carefully.

SKATEBOARDER: I'm really very sorry. Honestly.

— **The doctor wants to call**
  ☐ another doctor
  ☐ an ambulance.
— **Paula then walks**
  ☐ very slowly ☐ very quickly.

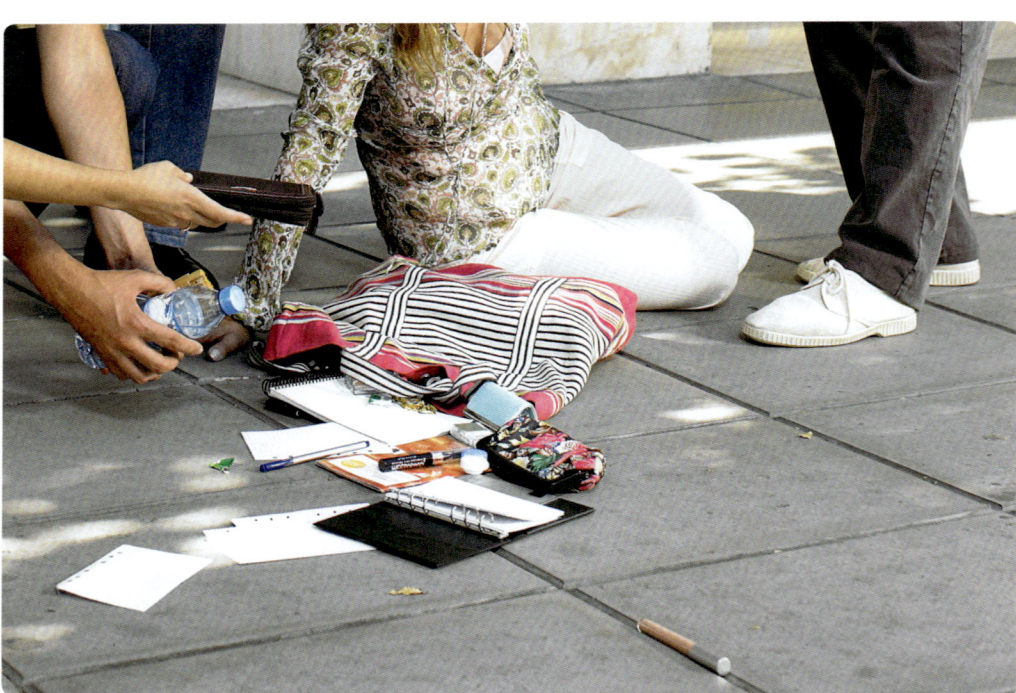

Wortschatz zum Dialog

◉ 123

to **hit**
treffen, schlagen

painful
schmerzhaft

to **fall**
fallen

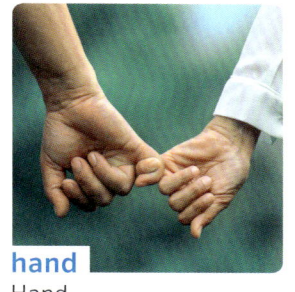

hand
Hand

ambulance
Krankenwagen

necessary
notwendig

slow
langsam

careful
vorsichtig

to **break**
brechen

wrist
Handgelenk

future
Zukunft

to **be lucky**
Glück haben

Der Körper

◎ 125

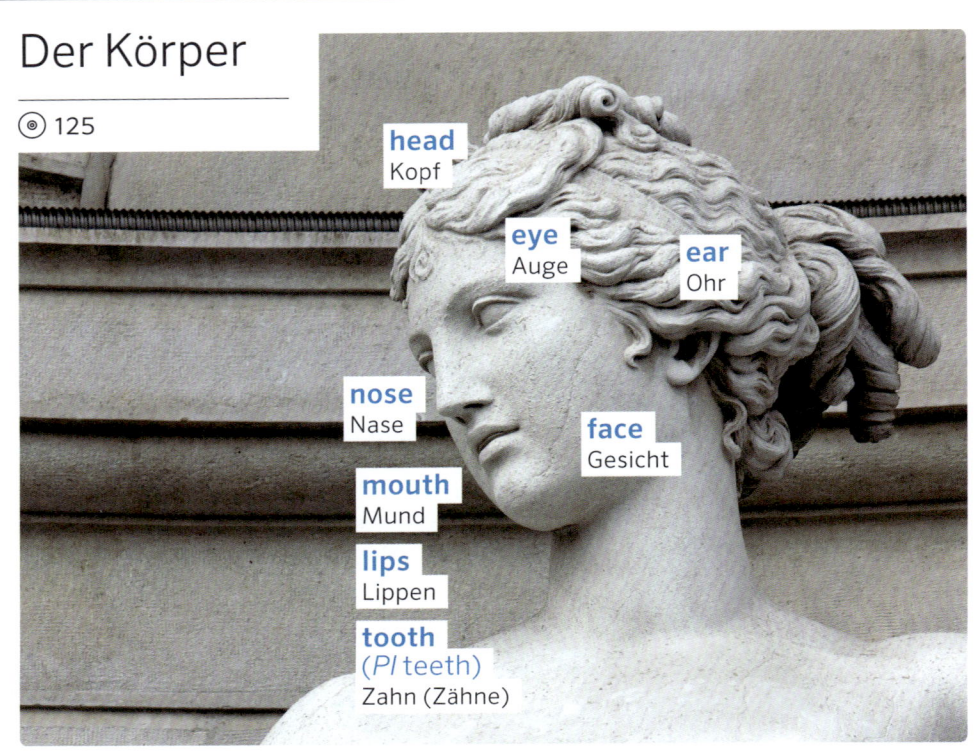

head
Kopf

eye
Auge

ear
Ohr

nose
Nase

face
Gesicht

mouth
Mund

lips
Lippen

tooth
(*Pl* teeth)
Zahn (Zähne)

body
Körper

shoulder
Schulter

back
Rücken

arm
Arm

leg
Bein

foot
(*Pl* feet)
Fuß (Füße)

hand
Hand

toe
Zeh

wrist
Hand-
gelenk

finger
Finger

1 Fügen Sie in die Tabelle die Körper- und Gesichtsteile ein, die der Mensch doppelt oder einzeln hat.

a double
eyes
....
....
....
....
....

b single
head
....
....
....
....
....

2 Welcher Begriff ist für die Aussage eher zutreffend? Unterstreichen Sie.

a My girlfriend's got green eyes / ears.

b His teeth / feet are perfectly straight.

c Her wrists / fingers are nice and long.

d His lips / shoulders are strong.

e Many Irish people have red legs / hair.

f Some people have six toes / faces.

g They've got round* faces / hands.

h Her arm / nose is small** and straight.

* round — rund; ** small — klein

3 Wie heißt das auf Englisch?

a left
links

b
schlagen

c
langsam

d
brechen

e
schmerzhaft

f
umstoßen

g
fallen

h
Krankenwagen

i
Bürgersteig

j
notwendig

Das *past progressive*

Mit dieser Zeitform, der <mark>Verlaufsform der Vergangenheit</mark>, beschreiben Sie ein Geschehen, das zu einem bestimmten Zeitpunkt der Vergangenheit gerade verlief, d.h. <mark>noch nicht abgeschlossen war</mark>.

Wie die Verlaufsform der Gegenwart (siehe Kapitel 6) setzt sich die Verlaufsform der Vergangenheit aus einer Form von **to be** und der Grundform des Verbs mit der Endung **-ing** zusammen. Für das *past progressive* wird **was(n't)/were(n't)** verwendet.

At midnight Tom was rowing on the river.

Um Mitternacht ruderte Tom auf dem Fluss.

Die Verlaufsform steht häufig auch bei einer Art <mark>Hintergrundhandlung</mark>, die gerade noch verläuft, bevor sie von einem <mark>neuen Ereignis unterbrochen</mark> wird.

**Tom was rowing on the river
when Brian jumped into the water.**

*Tom ruderte (gerade) auf dem Fluss,
als Brian ins Wasser sprang.*

Die Unterbrechung wird oft mit **when** (*als*) eingeleitet. Im **when**-Satz steht die <mark>einfache Vergangenheit</mark>.

Achtung: Im Englischen steht vor **when** kein Komma!

Adverbien der Art und Weise

Adverbien der Art und Weise drücken aus, wie etwas getan wird, während Adjektive beschreiben, wie etwas ist.

Man bildet Adverbien der Art und Weise, indem man an ein Adjektiv die Endung -ly anhängt.

She is an awful singer.
Sie ist eine schreckliche Sängerin.

She sings awfully.
Sie singt schrecklich.

REGELN ZUR ADVERBBILDUNG	ADJEKTIV	ADVERB
Die Endung -le + -ly wird zu -ly.	**terrible** *fürchterlich*	**terribly** *fürchterlich*
Die Endung **Konsonant + -y + -ly** wird zu **Konsonant + -ily**.	**happy** *glücklich*	**happily** *glücklich*
Die Endung -ic + -ly wird zu -ically.	**fantastic** *fantastisch*	**fantastically** *fantastisch*

Einige Adverbien haben die gleiche Form wie die Adjektive, zum Beispiel:

fast – *schnell*
late – *spät*
hard – *hart*

Achtung – das Adverb von **good** lautet **well**:

Philip is a good driver.
Philip ist ein guter Fahrer.

He drives very well.
Er fährt sehr gut.

4

Bilden Sie Adverbien von diesen Adjektiven und vervollständigen Sie die Sätze.

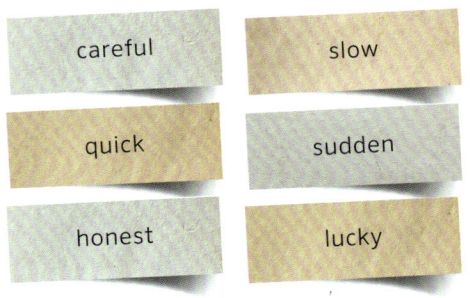

careful	slow
quick	sudden
honest	lucky

a _Suddenly_ someone knocked Paula down from behind.

b .... she didn't break her leg.

c The doctor looks at Paula's arm and leg ....

d The young man is .... sorry about everything.

e Paula doesn't go home .... after the accident.

f She walks home very .... after the accident.

5

Beantworten Sie die Fragen mit den Vorgaben in Klammern.

a What were you doing yesterday morning? (check / e-mails / office)

I was checking my e-mails in the office yesterday morning.

b What was she doing yesterday afternoon? (plan / trip / America)

....

....

c What were they doing yesterday evening? (play / badminton / sports centre)

....

....

d What was he doing this morning? (tidy / room / home)

....

....

e What were you doing this afternoon? (do / shopping / Chapel Market)

....

....

6

◉ 126

Hören Sie die Gespräche zwischen Arzt und Patienten und notieren Sie die wichtigsten Informationen.

Beschwerden:	Behandlung:
1	1 ....
....	....
....	....
....	....
2	2 ....
....	....
....	....
....	....
3	3 ....
....	....
....	....
....	....

7

Ergänzen Sie die Sätze. Ein Verb steht jeweils im *past progressive* (Hintergrund-situation), das andere im *simple past* (Unterbre-chung).

a We *were walking* .... (walk) to the pub when it *started* .... (start) to rain.

b Sheila .... (cook) dinner when we .... (arrive) home.

c When we .... (see) you at the cinema, ... (you, wait) for anyone?

d I .... (watch) television when Paula .... (call) me.

e He .... (unpack) his suitcase when he .... (have) a great idea.

f Tony .... (leave) the office when he .... (meet) his old boss.

8

Ein schwerer Unfall in Upper Street. Lesen Sie den Zeitungsbericht und beantworten Sie die Fragen mündlich.

a What was Mrs Price doing yesterday afternoon?

b What happened then?

c Was her leg broken?

d Did they have to call a doctor?

e What else was hurt?

f What did the doctor do?

g What have the police done?

h What is a real problem?

Daily News

Accident in Upper Street

Mrs Jenny Price was shopping in Upper Street, Islington, with a friend yesterday afternoon when she was knocked down from behind by a young skateboarder. Her leg and her wrist were hurt. "I wasn't skating very fast," the skateboarder said. He was very sorry, but the other people said that he shouldn't be skating on the pavement. Luckily there was a doctor there. He looked at Mrs Price's leg. Her leg was broken and her wrist was very painful. The doctor called an ambulance and Mrs Price was taken to hospital.

Skateboarding on the pavement is a real problem. Most people say that skateboarders should stay at their halfpipe and not skate where there are other people who do not know that they are coming from behind. The police have talked to the young man who is honestly sorry about the accident.

17
AUF DEM POLIZEIREVIER

In diesem Kapitel lernen Sie

Gegenstände genau zu beschreiben →

einen Verlust bei der Polizei zu melden →

über abgeschlossene und zeitnahe Handlungen zu berichten →

Wortschatz zum Dialog

◎ 127

to end
enden; beenden

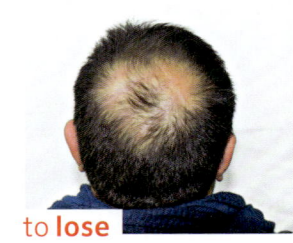

to lose
verlieren

wallet
Brieftasche

to steal
stehlen

biscuit
Keks

police station
Polizeirevier

officer
(Polizei)Beamter, Beamtin

telephone
Telefon

well
gut

to happen
geschehen, passieren

address
Adresse

number
Nummer

to describe
beschreiben

All's well that ends well!

◉ 128

Sheila Elton, Philip's mum, is at Mr Aziz's corner shop.

 **SHEILA:** Oh, I'm very sorry, but I think I've lost my wallet. Oh, where can it be? I had it with me when I left home. Maybe someone has stolen it.

 MR AZIZ: Here are your biscuits anyway. You can pay next time.

 Oh, I must go to the police station.

 I very much hope you find it.

At the police station.

 Good morning, officer. I think someone has stolen my wallet. This has never happened to me before. Or maybe I've lost it, I don't know.

 OFFICER: Well, could I have your name, address and telephone number first? And describe your wallet, please.

— Sheila has lost
  ☐ her cigarettes ☐ her wallet.
— Mr Aziz gives her the biscuits anyway. ☐ right ☐ wrong.

◉ 130

An *elderly* man comes in.

SHEILA: Black leather, with a bankcard and a credit card, about £20 and some photos of my family.

So maybe you left it on a park bench.

OFFICER: Now, Mrs Elton, when did you last have your wallet?

MAN: Officer, perhaps I can help you. I've just found a black leather wallet on a bench in the park. Perhaps it's yours?

I had it when I left home this morning at 10 o'clock. I know that. I went to the park for an hour or so. Then I went to Mr Aziz's shop to buy some biscuits. And my wallet was gone.

Oh, that's wonderful! Yes, it's mine! Thank you so much.

And did you take it out in the park?

Yes, I wanted to see how much money I had.

— Sheila's wallet is
☐ black leather ☐ brown leather.
— Sheila left home at
☐ nine o'clock ☐ ten o'clock.

?

Wortschatz zum Dialog

◎ 129

black
schwarz

leather
Leder

credit card
Kreditkarte

family
Familie

money
Geld

elderly
ältere(r, s)

bench
(Park)Bank

mine
mein(e)

bankcard
Bankkarte

about
etwa, ungefähr

last
zuletzt

to be gone
weg sein,
verschwunden sein

yours
dein(e), Ihr(e)

Farben

⊚ 131

yellow
gelb

red
rot

green
grün

blue
blau

grey
grau

orange
orangefarben

brown
braun

black
schwarz

white
weiß

blond(e)
blond

redheaded
rothaarig

dark-haired
dunkelhaarig

purple
purpurfarben

1 Benennen Sie die jeweilige Farbe.

a The colour of my car is ● ....*blue*.......... .

b My favourite colour is ● ....

c Bananas* are ● .... and

d tomatoes** are ● ....

e My mother is .... (blond), but

f my father's got .... (dunkel) hair.

g I love old ● .... and
○ .... photographs.

h The American spelling*** of
● .... is "gray".

*banana — *Banane*; **tomato — *Tomate*;
***spelling — *Schreibweise*

2 Finden Sie neun weitere Farben in der Wortschlange:

CNDHDI**YELLOW**DEIWRDKFODNEN
DUUZBLUEDBRYOKEUDKKINUUER
WREDDKWIUZZABOTDKDIESUZTTZ
GREENYXFSGREYSLIGJIKOIPBLACK
UGJURHZZRWHITEDKIZTUHDDEZZ
HBDTBVVTYFRJHJNZORANGEFKMV
NHFTRBROWNPLGOTHIUZTGEDJDJ
EJBBDEPURPLEDHDEJJENDUFHZH
TTDKNNFJUZDEZZTFHKWRDCSVE

3 Wie heißt das auf Englisch?

a *telephone*
Telefon

b ....
Leder

c ....
Familie

d ....
älter

e ....
(Park)Bank

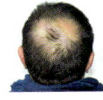

f ....
Geld

g ....
stehlen

h ....
enden

i ....
verlieren

j ....
mein

Das present perfect und das *simple past*

Das deutsche Perfekt ist dem *present perfect* von der Form her ganz ähnlich. Es gibt aber wichtige Unterschiede im Gebrauch in beiden Sprachen.

Sie wissen bereits, dass das *present perfect* bei Handlungen steht, die in der Vergangenheit angefangen haben und entweder noch nicht abgeschlossen sind oder noch Auswirkungen auf die Gegenwart haben (siehe Kapitel 15).

Someone has stolen my wallet.

Jemand hat meine Brieftasche gestohlen. (Der Dieb hat sie jetzt.)

SIMPLE PAST

Wird ein Zeitpunkt oder eine abgeschlossene Zeitspanne in der Vergangenheit genannt, müssen Sie im Englischen immer die einfache Vergangenheit verwenden, während im Deutschen auch da das Perfekt stehen kann.

PRESENT PERFECT

Beim *present perfect* wird kein Zeitpunkt in der Vergangenheit genannt. Häufig ist er zudem unbekannt oder unwichtig. Nur das Ergebnis für die Gegenwart ist relevant.

Emma has just escaped from the zoo.
Emma ist gerade aus dem Zoo entwischt.

Tom waited there at three o'clock.
Tom hat dort um drei Uhr gewartet.

Die folgenden Signalwörter zeigen Ihnen, welche Vergangenheitsform Sie brauchen:

SIMPLE PAST (BESTIMMTE ZEIT)	
yesterday	*gestern*
last …	*letzte(r, n) …*
… ago	*vor …*
at (+ Uhrzeit)	*um …*
on (+ Wochentag)	*am …*
in (+ Monat/Jahr)	*im/in …*

PRESENT PERFECT (UNBESTIMMTE ZEIT)	
ever	*jemals*
just	*gerade eben*
not yet	*noch nicht*
already	*schon*
before	*vor, vorher*
always	*immer*
so far	*bisher*

Alleinstehende Possessivpronomen

Possessivpronomen können nicht nur zusammen mit einem Substantiv verwendet werden, sie können auch alleine stehen. Im Englischen brauchen Sie dann allerdings eine andere Form:

POSSESSIV-PRONOMEN	… ALLEIN-STEHEND
my	mine
your	yours
his	his
her	hers
its	its
our	ours
your	yours
their	theirs

Do you like our cat?
Magst du unsere Katze?

It's not yours. It's mine!
Das ist nicht eure. Das ist meine!

4

Lesen Sie Sheilas E-Mail an Colin. Fassen Sie den Inhalt auf Deutsch zusammen.

New Message

To: westcol@jannimail.co.uk

Cc:

Subject: Thank You

From: shee.la@bo…   Signature: None

Dear Colin,

I want to thank you once again for taking my wallet to the police station. It is good to know that some people are honest. And the coffee together was very nice. We must go and have coffee again some time. I like the Coffee House in Upper Street very much. As for my family, my son Philip works in Islington and my grandson Andy goes to school. My husband died* ten years ago. Sometimes I feel lonely in this big house. I look forward to getting an e-mail from you.

Sheila

*to die — *sterben*

5

Unterstreichen Sie die richtigen Pronomen.

a Mine/My computer isn't working. Can I use your/yours?

b Sheila has lost her/hers wallet in the park.

c That's not your/yours car. It's our/ours.

d Theirs/Their is cheap. Your/Yours is expensive.

e My biscuit is nicer than yours/your.

f It wasn't Philip's car. It was my/mine.

g I'm buying my/mine ticket and Peter and Jackie are buying their/theirs.

6

◉ 132

Hören Sie das Gespräch auf dem Polizeirevier und korrigieren Sie die Aussagen.

a Mrs Cook has lost her bag.
Someone has stolen
Mrs Cook's bag.

b It has happened to her once before.
....
....

c Her bag is black leather with a bankcard and about £10 in it.
....
....

d Mrs Cook was sitting in a café.
....
....

e The money is still in the bag.
....
....

f The police officer gives her bag back immediately.
....
....

bag – Tasche

7

Present perfect oder *simple past* — welche Zeitform brauchen Sie?

a This morning Sheila *went* ....(go) to the park at 10 o'clock.

b She thinks that someone .... (steal) her wallet.

c This .... (never happen) to her before.

d She ....(go) to the corner shop to buy some biscuits.

e She ....(take) the wallet out in the park.

f Maybe she ....(leave) it on the park bench.

g Mr West: I ....(just find) a black leather wallet.

8

Verbinden Sie die folgenden englischen Begriffe mit der passenden Farbe.

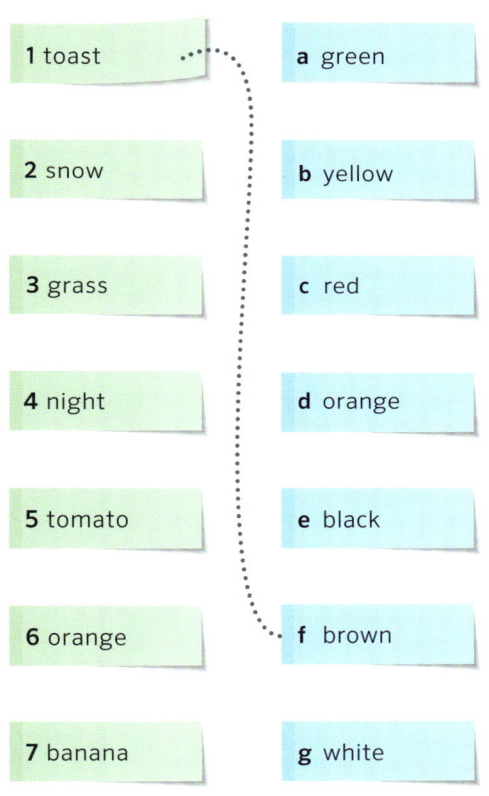

1 toast	**a** green
2 snow	**b** yellow
3 grass	**c** red
4 night	**d** orange
5 tomato	**e** black
6 orange	**f** brown
7 banana	**g** white

9

Bilden Sie Sätze in der Vergangenheit und sprechen Sie sie laut vor. Die Zeitform (*present perfect* oder *simple past*) kommt auf das Signalwort an. Achten Sie auch auf die richtige Position der Adverbien.

a already / some work / do / Philip.
Philip has already done some work.

b I / yesterday / my mother / see.

c Jenny / at ten o'clock / at the station / arrive.

d last Friday / we / to the theatre / go.

e the wallet / they / not yet / find.

f to see the doctor / I / on Thursday / my son / take.

18

EIN AUSFLUG

In diesem Kapitel lernen Sie

Vorschläge zu machen und Möglichkeiten zu besprechen →

um Bestätigung und Zustimmung zu bitten →

Vorlieben und Abneigungen zu äußern →

Wortschatz zum Dialog

◉ 133

to explore
erkunden, auskundschaften

beautiful
schön

to study
studieren

university
Universität

to park
parken

college
College, Akademie

town
(Klein)Stadt

guided tour
Führung

to suggest
vorschlagen

by
mit *(bei Verkehrs-mitteln)*

(was) founded
(wurde) gegründet

century
Jahrhundert

way
hier: Art und Weise

to go on
hier: teilnehmen

Exploring
new places

◉ 134

PHILIP: I'd very much like to show you Cambridge. It's one of the most beautiful cities in Britain.

PAULA: You didn't study there, did you?

No, I went to Manchester University. Good place. I liked living there.

When do you suggest going?

How about this Saturday? It's better to go by train, then you don't have any parking problems.

Tell me about the university. It's very old, isn't it?

Yes, the first college, Peter-house, was founded in the 13th century. The best way to see everything is just to walk round the centre of town. Or go on a guided tour.

— Philip studied
  ☐ at Cambridge University
  ☐ at Manchester University.
— The first college was founded
  ☐ in the 12th century
  ☐ in the 13th century.

?

◉ 136

 PAULA: I don't like going on guided tours, do you?

 PHILIP: Well, you can learn a lot, and we only have one day. Are you interested in seeing King's College Chapel — and the Backs and the Market?

 Yes, of course. But what are the Backs?

 Well, the backs of the colleges, by the river. You can take a punt and punt along the river and see all the most famous colleges.

 And what's a punt, Philip?

 It's a boat and you use a long pole to push the boat and yourself along.

 Oh, I know. They have punts on the river near Stuttgart. And sometimes you fall in the water, don't you?

 I don't, Paula. I must look up the times of the trains.

— Paula ☐ likes ☐ doesn't like guided tours.
— Philip falls in the water. ☐ right ☐ wrong

Wortschatz zum Dialog

◉ 135

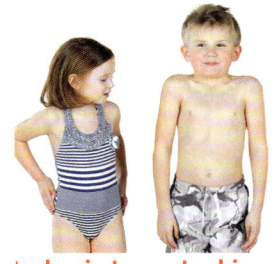

to **be interested in**
interessiert sein an

chapel
Kapelle

river
Fluss

punt
Stocherkahn

to **use**
benutzen

long
lang

pole
Stange, Pfahl

to **push**
schieben, drücken

to **look up**
nachschlagen

back
Rückseite; Rücken

to **punt**
staken

Kleidung

◉ 137

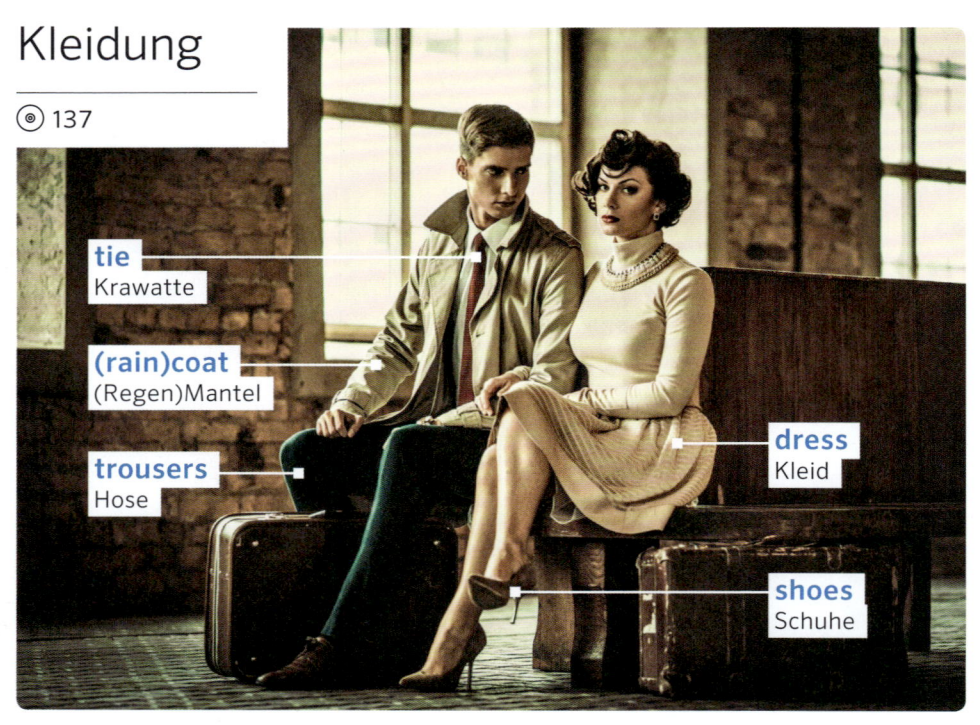

tie
Krawatte

(rain)coat
(Regen)Mantel

trousers
Hose

dress
Kleid

shoes
Schuhe

shirt
Hemd

jacket
Jackett,
Blazer

suit
Anzug;
Kostüm

umbrella
Regenschirm

tights
Strumpfhose

cardigan
Strickjacke

scarf
Schal,
Halstuch

jumper
Pullover

blouse
Bluse

skirt
Rock

1 Verbinden Sie das englische mit dem deutschen Wort.

a cardigan

b tie

c tights

d dress

e suit

1 Strumpfhose

2 Anzug

3 Krawatte

4 Strickjacke

5 Kleid

2 Finden Sie elf weitere Kleidungsstücke im Buchstabengitter.

D	S	E	S	U	I	T	O	P
A	K	D	D	D	E	R	M	N
T	I	E	C	S	H	O	E	S
G	R	D	Y	X	D	U	T	C
H	T	I	G	H	T	S	H	A
Z	B	L	O	U	S	E	D	R
T	L	J	S	H	I	R	T	F
F	Y	K	D	R	E	S	S	Q
C	A	R	D	I	G	A	N	Y
V	J	U	M	P	E	R	D	E
F	E	W	E	W	O	V	D	W

3 Wie heißt das auf Englisch?

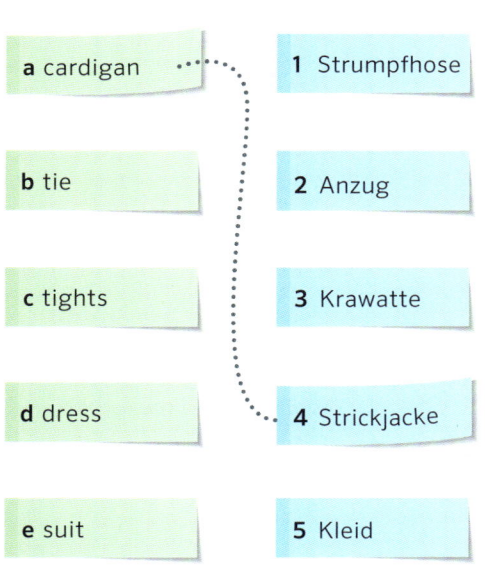

a *river*
Fluss

b
schön

c
parken

d
(Klein)Stadt

e
benutzen

f
nachschlagen

g
Stange, Pfahl

h
lang

i
schieben

j
erkunden

Das Gerund (II)

Sie haben in Kapitel 8 gelernt, dass ein Verb mit der Endung **-ing** zu einem Substantiv wird, das Gerund heißt. Es kann Subjekt oder Objekt sein und steht häufig nach Verben des Mögens oder Nicht-Mögens.

In der folgenden Übersicht haben wir für Sie weitere Wendungen zusammengestellt, mit denen Sie eine Vorliebe oder Abneigung ausdrücken können. Sie sehen, dass das nicht nur Verben sind, sondern auch Adjektive mit Präpositionen. Auf alle diese Wendungen folgt im Englischen ein Gerund.

I **hate** cooking.
Ich hasse Kochen.

He **loved** cooking.

VERBEN DES MÖGENS UND NICHT-MÖGENS + GERUND	
can't stand	*nicht ausstehen können*
don't mind	*nichts dagegen haben*
to like	*mögen, gern haben*
to love	*sehr gern machen*
to hate	*hassen, überhaupt nicht mögen*
to enjoy	*mögen, genießen*
to prefer	*vorziehen*
to dislike	*nicht mögen*

That's not how you **practise** cooking.

SONSTIGE VERBEN + GERUND	
to suggest	*vorschlagen*
to imagine	*sich vorstellen*
to practise	*üben*

He **looks forward to** cooking.

VERB + PRÄPOSITION + GERUND	
to look forward to	*sich freuen auf*
to thank for	*danken für*
to think about/of	*nachdenken über/ denken an*

He **stops** cooking.

VERBEN DES BEGINNENS, FORTSETZENS, BEENDENS + GERUND	
to begin	*anfangen*
to start	*starten*
to finish	*beenden*
to stop	*aufhören*

He is good
at cooking.

We have to
clean after
cooking.

ADJEKTIV + PRÄPOSITION + GERUND	
crazy about	verrückt nach
good at	gut in
bad at	schlecht in
famous for	berühmt für
interested in	interessiert an
be fond of	sehr gern haben
be keen on	sehr mögen

ALLEINSTEHENDE PRÄPOSITIONEN + GERUND	
after	nach
before	vor
without	ohne
instead of	(an)statt

Frageanhängsel

Um von Ihrem Gegenüber eine Bestätigung zu erfragen, brauchen Sie im Englischen ein question tag (Frageanhängsel).

Beachten Sie, dass bei einem bejahten Aussagesatz ein verneintes Frageanhängsel und bei einem verneinten Aussagesatz ein bejahtes Frageanhängsel angehängt wird.

It's beautiful, isn't it?
Sie ist wunderschön, nicht wahr?

It wasn't expensive, was it?
Sie war nicht teuer, oder?

4

◉ 138

Hören Sie das Gespräch zwischen Hazel und Kevin und notieren Sie die wichtigsten Informationen in Stichpunkten.

Where? *Oxford*

....

....

....

....

When? ....

....

....

....

....

....

What? ....

....

....

....

....

....

5

Familie Elton: Ergänzen Sie das passende Gerund.

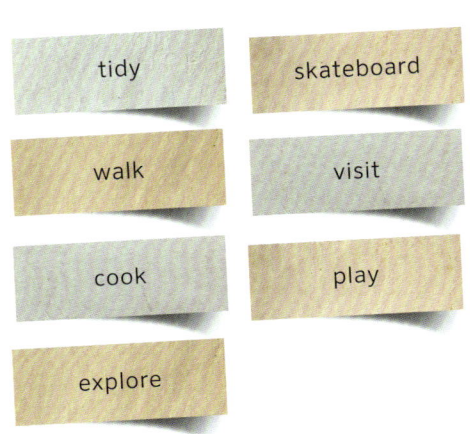

tidy	skateboard
walk	visit
cook	play
explore	

a *Exploring* .... new places is always fascinating.

b Sheila enjoys .... in the park.

c Philip is not very good at .... badminton.

d Andy is crazy about ....

e He can't stand .... up his room at home.

f Paula is looking forward to .... Cambridge very much.

g Philip is not very good at .... but he sometimes does the Sunday roast.

6

Lesen Sie den Werbetext über Cambridge und setzen Sie die passenden Verbformen (Gerund oder Infinitiv) ein. Es kann mehrere Lösungen geben.

walk / punt / go / visit / explore / see / learn

COME TO CAMBRIDGE!

Cambridge is one of the most beautiful cities in Britain. It is fascinating (a) _to see/visit/explore_ new places, so why not go to Cambridge. It's better (b) .... by train from London, then you don't have any parking problems. The University is very old. The first college, Peterhouse, was founded in the thirteenth century. The best way (c) .... everything is just (d) .... round the centre of town. Or go on a guided tour. You can (e) .... a lot on a guided tour if you only have one day. Are you interested in (f) .... King's College Chapel and (g) .... to the Market in the city centre? Or you can enjoy (h) .... along the river and (i) .... all the most famous colleges from the Backs. Look up the times of the trains now. We're sure you'll really love (j) .... Cambridge.

7

Ergänzen Sie das passende Frageanhängsel.

a It's nice there, _isn't it_?

b It isn't very far, ...?

c I don't like baked beans with everything, ... ?

d You didn't go to Cambridge, ...?

e There is a train every hour, ...?

f There are guided tours of the city ....?

8

Setzen Sie die Verben in die
jeweils richtige Zeitform.

* finally — *schließlich*
**to get away from sth. —
  etw. entkommen

Dear Mum and Dad,

I've got great news! Yesterday we went
(a) .... (punt) in Cambridge. What a
beautiful town! In the evening Philip and Sheila
(b) .... (invite) me over for a glass of
wine and (c) .... (ask) me if I'd like
(d) .... (move) into their house. They
(e) .... (have got) a free room in the
attic which is a lot nicer than the uncomfortable
B&B I (f) .... (live) in right now. And
I'd finally* (g) .... (**get away from)
all those baked beans. With the job everything is fine and I think I (h) ....
(stay) in England for some more time ;-)

All the best
Paula

Abschlusstest

1 Bilden Sie Fragen mit *will/won't* zu diesen Antworten.

---

a Yes, the trip will be in September.

....

....

b No, the hotel won't be very expensive.

....

....

c Yes, the conference will last two days.

....

....

d No, they won't have time for everything.

....

....

e Yes, the information will be ready in an hour.

....

....

f Yes, I'll have a coffee after that.

....

....

⚪ **von 6 Punkten**

2 Welche Form ist richtig? Kreuzen Sie an.

a Paula's leg hurts
- ☐ awful
- ☐ awfully
- ☐ most awful.

b The young man is
- ☐ terrible
- ☐ more terrible
- ☐ terribly
sorry.

c He was skating very
- ☐ fast
- ☐ faster
- ☐ fastest.

d Paula will walk
- ☐ slower
- ☐ slow
- ☐ slowly.

e She plays badminton
- ☐ fantastic
- ☐ fantastically
- ☐ fascinating.

f She speaks English very
- ☐ good
- ☐ better
- ☐ well.

 von 6 Punkten

3 Welches Hilfsverb passt? Kreuzen Sie es an.

a We're late. We
- ☐ may
- ☐ can
- ☐ must
hurry.

b You
- ☐ mustn't
- ☐ should
- ☐ must
do that!
It's dangerous.

c We
- ☐ should
- ☐ needn't
- ☐ could
see everything in one
day. It's too much.

d We
- ☐ mustn't
- ☐ would
- ☐ should
get the information
Mr Butler wants.

e What
- ☐ would
- ☐ needn't
- ☐ should
you like to see?

f We
- ☐ can't
- ☐ needn't
- ☐ have to
check in over there.
Come on, it's late.

von 6 Punkten

4 Ergänzen Sie die passenden Frageanhängsel.

a The university is very old, ...?

b There's a lot to see in New York, ...?

c The conference isn't in New York, ...?

d Paula can't find a flat, ...?

e It would be better to take a taxi, ...?

f That was much better, ...?

von 6 Punkten

5 Lesen Sie den Text und notieren Sie die Informationen.

Flights from London go to Terminal 7 of John F. Kennedy International Airport. It is a very big airport. In America the first thing to do is to pick up your rental car. You have to ask where the car rental counters are. There you have to show your voucher and your driver's license. Then you take the shuttle that runs from AirTrain Station C. The rental car offices are on the Van Wyck Expressway, which is near the entrance to the airport. There you can pick up your car keys. They will show you your car and answer any questions you have. All the cars have a navigation system, so it is easy to find your hotel or the place where you want to go.

a Pick up what? ....

....

b Show what? ....

....

c Shuttle from where? ....

....

d Rental car offices where? ....

....

e Pick up what there? ....

....

f How to find your hotel? ....

....

○ **von 6 Punkten**

6 Was ist richtig? Kreuzen Sie an.

a ☐ Explore
☐ Explored
☐ Exploring
new places is fun.

b I am looking forward to
☐ see
☐ seeing
☐ saw
Cambridge.

c Philip enjoys
☐ visiting
☐ visited
☐ visit
new places.

d I'd like
☐ going
☐ to go
☐ go
on a guided tour.

e I want
☐ taking
☐ takeaway
☐ to take
a punt out on the river.

f We must
☐ to look up
☐ look up
☐ looking up
the train times on the Internet.

○ **von 6 Punkten**

7 Was sagen Sie, wenn …

a ... Sie fragen möchten, ob wir das nicht jetzt machen könnten?

b ... Sie sagen wollen, dass wir nur einmal umsteigen müssen?

c ... Sie sagen wollen, dass wir dort drüben einchecken müssen?

d ... Sie fragen möchten, wo man hingehen soll?

e ... Sie sagen möchten, dass wir ein Mietauto abholen möchten?

f ... Sie sagen möchten, dass Sie noch nie in einem solchen Hotel übernachtet haben?

g ... Sie sagen wollen, dass Sie sich auf ein richtiges amerikanisches Frühstück freuen?

h ... Sie sagen möchten, dass Sie eine Tasse Tee mit viel Zucker machen werden?

von 8 Punkten

8 Sie hören drei Dialoge. Notieren Sie die Stadt, um die es geht und eine der Sehenswürdigkeiten, die erwähnt werden.

◉ 139

1 Stadt & Sehenswürdigkeit

....

....

2 Stadt & Sehenswürdigkeit

....

....

3 Stadt & Sehenswürdigkeit

....

....

von 6 Punkten

Sie haben

Punkte von 50 erreicht.

BEWERTUNG

45–50
★★★★
Very good
Kompliment! Ihre Mühe hat sich wirklich gelohnt.

35–44
★★★ Good
Prima — Sie haben sehr viel gelernt!

25–34
★★ OK
Vieles klappt schon ziemlich gut, aber üben Sie weiter an den Stellen, die Ihnen noch Schwierigkeiten bereiten.

Weniger als 25
★ You can do better
Sie haben durchgehalten — klasse! Sie können es aber sicherlich noch besser, und es lohnt sich bestimmt, nochmals die Kapitel zu wiederholen, die Sie noch nicht so gut können.

ANHANG

Im Anhang finden Sie

die Lösungen zu den
Aufgaben →

Hinweise zur
Grammatik und zur
Aussprache →

ein Gesamtverzeichnis
der Vokabeln →

LÖSUNGEN

BEGRÜSSUNG

Fragen zum Dialog ....
Teil 1: Germany — Stuttgart
Teil 2: isn't — isn't

1 ....
a 1 Hi, David, how are you?
   2 Good morning, Ms Holm,
   I'm fine, thanks. 3 OK, see
   you soon. 4 Bye bye, Ms
   Holm.
b 1 Good afternoon, I'm Ellen.
   2 Hi, Ellen, nice to meet you.
   My name is Henry. 3 Where
   are you from? 4 I'm from
   Germany.

2 ....
a name   c meet   e you
b Hello   d Nice   f thanks

3 ....
a office   f morning
b head   g Welcome!
c to come   h to talk
d to go   i here
e new   j we

4 ....
a you, I   c It   e They
b She   d He   f We

5 ....
a we aren't; we're not
b he isn't; he's not
c you aren't; you're not
d I'm not
e she isn't; she's not
f they aren't; they're not
g it isn't; it's not

6 ....
a 're   d 's   g 's   j 'm
b 'm   e 's   h 's   k 're
c 's   f 's   i 're

7 ....
a Paula Schneider isn't from
  England. *Auch möglich:*
  Paula Schneider's not from
  England.
b She isn't / She's not from
  Munich.
c I'm not the Head of
  Marketing.
d Mr Butler isn't / Mr Butler's
  not a computer expert.
e We aren't / We're not OK this
  morning.
f They aren't / They're not in
  Mr Butler's office.
g Hazel, you aren't / Hazel,
  you're not the Head
  of Marketing.
h This isn't Mr Butler's
  computer.

8 ....
Hazel: Hi, Kevin. How are you
today?
Kevin: Gut, danke. *Fine,
thanks.*
Hazel: This is Paula.
Kevin: Hello, Paula. Schön, Sie
kennenzulernen. *Nice to meet
you.*
Paula: Hello, Kevin.
Kevin: Woher kommen Sie?
Where are you from?
Paula: I'm from Stuttgart — in
the south of Germany.
Kevin: Oh, yes. Ich kenne Stutt-
gart. Es ist schön. *I know
Stuttgart. It's nice.*
Hazel: And this is Jenny.
Jenny: Hi, Paula. Schön, Sie
hier bei uns zu haben. *Nice to
have you with us.*
Paula: Hello, Jenny. Nice to
meet you, too.
Jenny: Willkommen in England!
Welcome to England!
Paula: Thanks.

KENNENLERNEN
UND SMALL TALK

Fragen zum Dialog ....
Teil 1: coffee — no
Teil 2: projects — every day —
     never

1 ....
a boring   e team
b phone   f work
c e-mails   g check
d colleague

2 ....
a two   f fifteen
b four   g twenty-two
c seven   h thirty-one
d nine   i forty
e eleven   j fifty-six
*(Achtung: „four"— aber „forty"
ohne „u"!)*

3 ....
a at home   f to say
b lunch   g sugar
c people   h milk
d to drink   i typical
e hour   j the same

4 ....
a your   c my   e Her
b our   d His   f their

5 ....
Individuelle Antworten, z. B.:
a I never drink coffee.
b I sometimes drink tea with
  milk.
c I always answer my e-mails,
  too.
d I sometimes drink coffee at
  work.
e I often work at home.

6 ....
a 3   b 5   c 2   d 4   e 1

7 ....
a drink   e have
b check   f get
c drink   g gets
d talks

276

8
a Coffee, but no milk.
b Tea with milk.
c Coffee with sugar.
d Tea, but no sugar and no milk.

9
a office
b meetings
c computers
d week
e e-mails
f hour

3

ÜBER SICH SELBST SPRECHEN

Fragen zum Dialog
Teil 1: not happy — a new computer
Teil 2: wrong — Scotland.

1
a sister
b wife
c grandfather
d aunt
e daughter
f nephew
g father

2
1 b
2 e
3 c
4 a
5 d

3
a honest
b happy
c school
d upstairs
e dead
f old
g evening
h uncomfortable
i surprised
j expensive

4
a Yes, I have.
b No, I can't.
c Yes, she has.
d Yes, he has.
e No, they aren't
f Yes, I am.
g No, I'm not / No, you aren't
h No, he isn't

5
a Does, doesn't
b Does, doesn't
c Does, does
d Do, Yes, I do./No, I don't.

6
a son's
b computers
c colleague's
d computers
e mum's
f computers

7
Ausspracheübung

8
a Philip's
b He's, years
c lives
d feels, wants
e She's
f wants
g interests
h It's
i meets
j It's
k She's
l Everything's
m landlady's
n flats
o Philip's

9
a coffee
b people
c usually
d Welcome
e meeting
f Germany
g England
h hour
i answer

Lösungswort: colleague

10
a I don't drink coffee every morning.
b We don't like our B&B in London.
c She doesn't always say thank you.
d You don't look happy today.
e They don't have time this evening.
f Philip doesn't find his computer.
g Mum doesn't want to meet people.

4

KULTURELLE UNTERSCHIEDE

Fragen zum Dialog
Teil 1: isn't — at the bar
Teil 2: cook — twelve o'clock.

1
a thirty-first
b fifth
c fourth
d first
e twenty-second
f eighth

2
a photographer
b fabric
c poison
d to get
e sensible
f plant
g gift
h photograph
i well-behaved

3
a different
b cook, chef
c to close
d to pay
e waiter
f difficult
g mobile (phone)
h last
i drink
j real

4
a There is
b There are
c There are
d There is
e There are
f There are

5
1 3 am
2 11 pm
3 8 am
4 5 am
5 9 pm
6 2 am

6
a first
b fourth
c eighth/last
d second
e seventh
f sixth
g third
h fifth

7
a Sekretärin
b Elektronik-firma
c Freizeit
d Sport
e Tennis
f Basketball
g Fußball
h Tanzen
i Disko
j Einkaufen
k Musik
l Gitarre

8
a No, there isn't a waiter.
b You get your drinks at the bar.
c You pay each time.
d You pay before you leave.
e She likes gin and tonic.
f The German word Handy means mobile.
g The English word chef means cook.
h The pub closes at twelve o'clock.

9
1 g
2 f
3 e
4 b
5 h
6 c
7 d
8 a

ZWISCHENTEST 1

1
a Nice to meet you.
b Welcome to England!
c What's wrong?
d Have you got time to go out this evening?
e Thank you very much.
f That's a great idea.
g What does that word mean?

→ *siehe Kapitel 4*

2
a Are   d is
b is   e am
c are   f are

→ *siehe Kapitel 1*

3
a Stuttgart.
b in their canteen.
c InterChip UK.
d for his interests.
e everything is wrong.
f they are expensive.

→ *siehe Kapitel 3*

4
a How   c Why   e What
b Where d Where f What

→ *siehe Kapitel 2*

5
a Stuttgart   c Islington
b London Road

→ *siehe Kapitel 4*

6
1 020 5412 6094
2 7843 2361
3 020 9481 4638

→ *siehe Kapitel 2*

7
a Does   c Does   e Does
b Does   d Do   f Do

→ *siehe Kapitel 3*

8
a Philip doesn't look very happy.
b Andy doesn't like school.
c Philip's mum feels lonely.
d She wants to meet people.
e Paula doesn't feel fine in her little room.
f She feels depressed.

→ *siehe Kapitel 3*

9
a Yes, I am.
b No, she can't.
c Yes, she does.
d Yes, it is.
e No, she can't.
f Yes, she has.

→ *siehe Kapitel 3*

5

EINKAUFEN

Fragen zum Dialog
Teil 1: right — some fruit
Teil 2: right — Italian coffee.

1
a street   d pound
b grocer   e buy
c fresh   f pays

2
a I want to buy four oranges, please.
b Could I have a pound of red apples, please?
c Have you got any Italian coffee?
d How much is it?

3
a half   f fruit
b lady   g market
c Italian   h to buy
d much   i any
e Sorry!   j date

4
a any, some   d some
b any, some   e any
c any   f some

5
a Enjoy your coffee!
b Buy the apples!
c Don't drink it!
d Find my computer!
e Don't leave the house at eight o'clock!
f Answer my question!

6
1 Grocer: Good morning. How are you?
2 Paula: I'm fine, thanks. How are you?
3 Grocer: I'm fine too. What would you like today?
4 Paula: Do you have any eggs?
5 Grocer: Yes, I do. And they're very fresh. Would you like some?
6 Paula: Yes. Could I have six, please? And do you have any tomatoes?
7 Grocer: I don't have any tomatoes today. Would you like some apples?
8 Paula: Yes, could I have a pound of red apples, please?
9 Grocer: Of course. That's £2.50 altogether.

7
— Mum's birthday is on the eleventh of November.
— Andy's birthday is on the thirteenth of February.
— My birthday is on the fifteenth of May.
— John's birthday is on the fifth of December.
— Hazel's birthday is on the second of March.
— Joyce's birthday is on the twenty-first of August.
— Mr Butler's birthday is on the seventeenth of May.
— I don't know when Paula's birthday is.

8
a She doesn't have any fresh fruit.
b Paula doesn't buy any tea
c They don't find any eggs at the market.
d Philip doesn't drink any coffee in the canteen.

e We don't check any e-mails at the office.
f He doesn't understand any words.

9

— **Grocer:** Good morning. How are you today? — **Kevin:** Fine, thanks. *I'd like some oranges, please.* — **Grocer:** The oranges aren't really fresh today. But we've got some lovely apples. — **Kevin:** *Have you got any English apples?* — **Grocer:** Yes, we've got some from the south of England. — **Kevin:** OK, I'll have some of those then. *How much are they?* — **Grocer:** £2.40 a pound. — **Kevin:** *Give me two pounds then.* — **Grocer:** That's £4.80. — **Kevin:** *And a packet of tea, please.* — **Grocer:** This one is very nice. It's £3.30. That's £8.10 altogether. — **Kevin:** Here's £10. — **Grocer:** And £1.90 for you. Thanks. — **Kevin:** *Thank you very much, and goodbye.*

IM RESTAURANT

Fragen zum Dialog ....
Teil 1: a soup — Italian red wine
Teil 2: German and Spanish — They go fifty-fifty.

1

a A bottle of water and some bread, please.
b Could you repeat that, please?
c What does that mean?
d How do you say that in English?
e Could you speak more slowly, please?

2

a understand	**e** in
b speak	**f** Sorry!
c Where	**g** that
d say	**h** mean

3

a table	**f** corner
b bill	**g** late
c to start	**h** starter
d window	**i** to speak
e to sit	**j** bottle

4

a is drinking	**d** am enjoying
b is having	**e** are doing
c is thinking	**f** are talking

5

a Paula and Philip are sitting by the window.
b They are having ravioli.
c They are drinking red wine.
d The people over there are speaking German.
e The people in the corner aretalking Spanish.
f The waiter is coming this way.

6

a him	**d** your
b my	**e** us
c she?	**f** They

7

— Where would you like to sit? *Over there by the window.*
— What would you like to have? *How about a starter?*
— And what would you like after that? *This salad looks very good.*
— And would you like some wine? *I like Italian red wines.*
— Can I have the bill, please? *Yes, of course. Just a minute, please.*
— Would you like to go to a pub now? *No, not today. It's late.*

8

a these	**e** that
b those	**f** that
c these	**g** these
d this	

9

a I'm drinking tea, too.
b I'm not planning any new projects.
c I'm not working at home.
d I'm answering my e-mails, too.

10

a these	**d** those
b those	**e** these
c This	**f** that

SEHENS-WÜRDIGKEITEN

Fragen zum Dialog ....
Teil 1: right — wrong
Teil 2: wrong — the Tower.

1

a at	**e** for
b at/in	**f** on
c from/in	**g** to
d in	

2

a boat trip	**e** famous
b Thames	**f** Tower
c ticket	**g** Crown Jewels
d deck	

3

a tower	**f** queue
b to hurry	**g** boat
c fun	**h** to decide
d to get off	**i** famous
e to stand	**j** inside

4

a Paula is going to check her e-mails tomorrow morning, too.
b I'm not going to take any photos tomorrow.
c We aren't/We're not going to meet any friends tomorrow evening.
d Philip's going to stay at home on Saturday, too.
e I'm / We're going to see the sights on Sunday, too.
f I'm not going to learn any Italian tomorrow.

5

a Sheila, Philip and Andy are going to have breakfast.
b Paula and Philip are going to meet at the ticket office.
c Philip is going to buy a ticket.

d They are going to sit on the open deck.
e They are going to get off at St. Paul's Cathedral.
f They are going to look at the Globe Theatre.

6

a office
b ticket
c deck
d inside
e sights
f Tower
g keep
h view
i Theatre
j performances
k everything

7

a must
b can't
c may
d can
e needn't
f mustn't / may not

8

a on
b before
c for
d in
e to
f by
g from
h in

9

a must
b must
c mustn't
d can
e must
f can't
g can
h can
i needn't

8
SPORT UND FREIZEIT

Fragen zum Dialog
Teil 1: rugby — badminton.
Teil 2: skateboarding — right

1

1 c	4 a
2 b	5 e
3 d	

2

Individuelle Antworten, z. B.:
a I like skiing,
I like to go swimming,
I like sailing,
I like hiking and skiing …
b I don't like cricket,
I don't like playing football,
I don't like fishing…

3

a homework
b afternoon
c to suppose
d accident
e together
f to play
g to hurt
h club
i dangerous
j lots of

4

a works, is working
b checks, is checking
c is ringing, rings and rings
d are having, have
e talks, is talking
f feels, is feeling

5

a herself
b themselves
c itself
d himself
e myself
f themselves
g yourself

6

1 d	3 b	5 c
2 e	4 a	

7

Simple present:
start, drinks, likes
Present progressive:
is playing, is phoning, is enjoying, is taking

8

— Football and cricket, I suppose.
— I can play badminton, but not very well.
— I like going for walks and sometimes I play Bingo.
— Skateboarding is best.
— There's a halfpipe not far from here.
— We have football and cricket at school.

9

a walks
b third
e July
f seventy
g dad
c Germany
d bacon
h those
i pound

Lösungswort: Wimbledon

9
NEUE FREUNDSCHAFTEN

Fragen zum Dialog
Teil 1: upstairs — maths homework
Teil 2: nicer — Indian takeaway

1

a Sunday
b August
c Tuesday
d October
e Monday
f May
g Friday

2

a 3	c 5	e 4
b 6	d 1	f 2

3

a to eat
b loud
c downstairs
d to forget
e to pour out
f flower
g quiet
h nose
i to enjoy
j crazy

4

a oldest
b bigger
c loud
d freshest
e better
f craziest
g nice
h quieter

5

a Friday — cinema
b Sunday — boat trip on the Thames
c Tuesday — maths homework
d Thursday — skateboard at the halfpipe

6

a louder
b quieter
c nicer
d better
e biggest
f oveliest

7

a (On Thursday) He is working later than usual (on Thursday)
b (On Friday) They're going to the cinema (on Friday).
c (On Saturday) We're going shopping at one of the markets (on Saturday).

d (On Sunday) She's going for a walk in one of the parks (on Sunday).

e (On Monday) I'm having lunch with Mr Butler (on Monday).

f (On Tuesday) Lisa is helping Andy with his homework (on Tuesday).

g (On Wednesday) They're meeting at the Globe Theatre (on Wednesday).

8 ....

a Philip is playing football at 10 o'clock on Sunday.

b On Friday evening he is going to the pub with Andy.

c At 11 o'clock on Thursday he is having a meeting with Joyce Marlow.

d On Tuesday Philip is buying a new computer.

e He is having dinner with Paula at Krishna's Restaurant on Saturday evening.

f On Friday afternoon Philip is showing Paula the offices.

g On Sunday evening he is calling Aunt Rosie.

10

ALLTAGS-PFLICHTEN

Fragen zum Dialog ....

Teil 1: listened to a concert. – badminton with Paula.

Teil 2: has got lots of things to do. – last week

1 ....

a bought   **e** took
b went   **f** met
c drank   **g** got
d found   **h** did

2 ....

a terrible
b September
c concert
d takeaway
e office
f age

3 ....

a concert   **f** gran
b woman   **g** unhappy
c to tidy up   **h** to watch
d to listen to   **i** mess
e again   **j** young

4 ....

a talked   **f** enjoyed
b enjoyed   **g** had
c preferred   **h** went
d liked   **i** did
e played

5 ....

a most uncomfortable/attractive
b most expensive/attractive
c more difficult/attractive
d more difficult/attractive
e more depressed

6 ....

— **Mum:** Who is going to do the boring chores in this house?
— **Lisa:** *I just haven't got the time, Mum.*
— **Mum:** I don't want to tidy up your room. It's an awful mess.
— **Lisa:** *And I don't want you to tidy up my things!*
— **Mum:** And who cleans the house? I need some help.
— **Lisa:** *Well, I could help you on Saturday.*
— **Mum:** And who does all the cooking?
— **Lisa:** *That's a better idea. I like cooking.*
— **Mum:** When was the last time you tidied up your room?
— **Lisa:** *Last week. OK, Mum, I can tidy it up a bit this evening.* — **Mum:** At least do it before Andy comes to see you. — **Lisa:** *Yes, Mum. Of course, Mum. He's coming tomorrow.*

7 ....

a awful   **e** terrible
b wonderful   **f** open
c Italian   **g** Spanish
d quiet

8 ....

— late, later, latest
— boring, more boring, most boring

— typical, more typical, most typical
— bad, worse, worst
— great, greater, greatest
— difficult, more difficult, most difficult
— young, younger, youngest
— good, better, best

11

FAMILIENLEBEN

Fragen zum Dialog ....

Teil 1: wrong – wrong
Teil 2: right – wrong

1 ....

a German   **e** German
b Spanish   **f** Italian
c French   **g** Portuguese
d English   **h** English

2 ....

a west   **e** north
b south   **f** east
c east   **g** west
d south   **h** north

3 ....

a vegetables   **f** to cook
b cheap   **g** city
c village   **h** potatoes
d garden   **i** to move
e to be born   **j** wonderful

4 ....

a ten sixty-six
b fifteen eighty-eight
c sixteen sixteen
d seventeen eighty-nine
e eighteen twelve
f nineteen forty
g nineteen sixty-eight
h nineteen ninety-nine
i twenty ten/two thousand and ten
j twenty thirty-two/two thousand and thirty-two

5 ....

a When was Sheila born?
b When did she move to Islington?
c Where was she born?
d Why didn't she go back to the country?

6 ....

Lösungsvorschlag:

a breakfast
b Mum
c most
d German/French/
American
e lamb/chicken
f lovely
g water, beer
h themselves

7 ....

a Andy never cooks the meals on Sundays.
b He always checks his e-mails in the morning.
c He often eats fruit from the market.
d Andy usually does his homework at Lisa's place in the evening.
e He tidied up his room yesterday morning.

8 ....

Individuelle Lösungen, z. B.:

a I was born in 1992.
b My family lived in Hamburg.
c We often had pasta on Sundays.
d My father stayed at home, but our mother worked in an office.
e My mother was from Dortmund.

9 ....

1 No, she wasn't.
She was born in 1940.
2 No, she didn't.
She lived in the country then.
3 No, he didn't.
He bought the house in 1947.
4 No, they didn't.
They moved to Islington in 1947.
5 No, it wasn't.
It was very different then.
6 No, she didn't.
She stayed in Islington.

ZT

ZWISCHENTEST 2

1 ....

a happier
b nice
c best
d depressed
e most uncomfortable
f more expensive

→ *siehe Kapitel 9, 10*

2 ....

a This is going to be fun.
b I can help you with your homework.
c What are you doing this weekend?
d Can't you turn the music down, please?
e I haven't got (any) time.
f Who is going to do the boring chores?
g When were you born?
h What is the food like in Germany?

→ *siehe Kapitel 11*

3 ....

a some   d any
b any   e anything
c some   f some

→ *siehe Kapitel 5*

4 ....

1 badminton —
Wednesday, 8 o'clock
2 walk in the park —
Sunday, 3 o'clock
3 boat trip on the Thames —
Tuesday, 2 o'clock

→ *siehe Kapitel 8, 9*

5 ....

a Tower of London —
Crown Jewels
b St. Paul's Cathedral —
fantastic view
c Globe Theatre —
Shakespeare performances

→ *siehe Kapitel 7*

---

6 ....

a went   d was
b did   e played
c had   f cooked

→ *siehe Kapitel 10*

7 ....

a What are they going to do?
b Andy is going to do some homework.
c Lisa is going to help him with it.
d Paula and Philip are going to play badminton next week.
e Philip is going to cook the Sunday roast.
f Sheila and Mahmoud aren't going to have coffee together today.

→ *siehe Kapitel 7*

8 ....

a you may not   e they must
b I can   f we needn't/
c she can't   don't have
d she can't   to

→ *siehe Kapitel 7*

12

EINE REISE PLANEN

Fragen zum Dialog ....

Teil 1: to the USA —
two days
Teil 2: for both of them. —
right

1 ....

a How   d When
b Where   e What
c Who   f How much

2 ....

Individuelle Lösungen, z. B.:

a I live in Potsdam, near Berlin.
b I prefer tea for breakfast.
c I went to bed at eleven o'clock.
d I drink three or four cups.
e Because I want to go to the United States.

3

a to give	**f** ready
b near	**g** centre
c free	**h** business trip
d later	**i** to hope
e flight	**j** to last

4

a cities
b USA
c trip
d would
e Building
f Fifth
g world
h Central
i website

5

a won't, will
b won't, will
c won't, will
d won't, will

6

a wrong
b wrong
c right
d right

7

Lösungsvorschlag:
a Shall — Yes, that's a good idea.
b Would — Yes, there's a (nice) café over there.
c Could/Would — Yes, of course I can/will.
d Let's — No, let's do it later.
e Shall/Shouldn't — Yes, that's a great idea.

8

a Chris will call the office this afternoon.
b James won't cook the potatoes
c They won't confirm the trip.
d We'll invite all our friends.
e I'll have some wine.
f You won't stay a bit longer.
g They'll eat in an expensive restaurant.

9

Ausspracheübung

13

VERKEHRSMITTEL

Fragen zum Dialog
Teil 1: the train — an alarm at the station
Teil 2: a taxi — clerks

1

a It's (a) quarter past nine/ nine fifteen.
b It's half past eleven/ eleven thirty.
c It's sixteen minutes past eight/eight sixteen.
d It's ten minutes to four/ three fifty.

2

a *What's* the time?
b *It's* twelve thirty o'clock.
c It's close to *midnight*.
d It's five *o'clock*.
e It's 9:30 — half *past nine*.
f It's 20 *past* 2 o'clock.
g It's 6:45 — three (a) quarter *to* seven.

3

a bus	**f** driver
b to miss	**g** traffic
c fast	**h** to leave
d suitcase	**i** train
e plane	**j** to run

4

a have to buy/get
b has to carry
c have to leave
d have to run/hurry
e have to hurry/run

5

Individuelle Antworten; z.B.:
a we'll take him with us.
b If the train isn't late,
c she'll have to find a flat.
d they won't catch the bus.
e If he hurries,
f we will have to invite Alfred, too.

6

a five to seven

b seven twenty-five
c half past eight
d seven forty-five
e quarter to seven

7

1 — 4 tickets
— Underground
— Heathrow
— £20 (£5 each)
2 — 1 ticket
— train
— Cambridge
— £27
3 — 3 tickets
— plane
— New York
— £897 (£299 each)
4 — 2 tickets
— boat
— Greenwich
— £18 (£9 each).

8

a No, they're not. They're expensive!
b No, it's not. It's very loud!
c No, she's not. She's so old!
d No, it wasn't. It was terrible/awful!
e No, it isn't. It's really small!
f No, he doesn't. He looks unhappy.

14

NACH DEM WEG FRAGEN

Fragen zum Dialog
Teil 1: New York. — in a red uniform
Teil 2: navigation system. — at the rental office

1

a get
b go/drive
c turn
d take
e left/right
f park
g behind

2

a 4   b 3
c 2   d 1

3

a to drive   f key
b strong   g to sign
c car   h company
d safe   i (on the)
e driver's   right
    license   j to tell

4

a which/that
b which/that
c who
d which/that
e which/that/
    kein Relativpronomen
f which/that/
    kein Relativpronomen

5

a Sheila called Philip, who was at the cinema.
b Andy has to pick up the car that he reserved.
c Stewart bought a coffee, which he drank immediately.
d Jo is writing an e-mail to Martin, who is in America.
e I am taking the train that goes to the airport.

6

a They picked up their car at JFK Airport.
b The conference centre is in the USA.
c After the conference they will drive back to JFK and then go to Manhattan.
d They have one day for the sights in Manhattan.
e Paula is going to write an e-mail to Mr Butler.

7

1 Turn left at the first traffic lights.
2 Turn right at the next crossroads.
3 Take the first turning on the left. Then it's only one minute's walk.
4 Go straight on. The station is on your left.

5 You are going the right way if you can see the restaurant on your right.
6 Take the second exit and drive straight on to the Conference Centre on the left.

8

a The taxi which/that took us to the station was very expensive.
b The man who gave them the keys was really old.
c The concert (which/that) I was at last week was fantastic.
d The shuttle which/that goes to the expressway was late.
e The woman who came to the office is our new colleague.
f The small coffee I bought was cold.

15

IM HOTEL

Fragen zum Dialog
Teil 1: in the foyer — wrong
Teil 2: wrong — right

1

a unpack   e remote
b wardrobe   control
c water   f TV
d hairdryer   g reception

2

a tap   e wardrobe
b chair   f shower
c toilet   Lösungswort:
d light   pillow

3

a light   f hot
b to repair   g floor
c American   h reception
d egg   i to arrive
e to begin   j shower

4

a have arrived
b have been
c have unpacked
d has called
e has looked

5

a Philip is phoning after the first morning of the conference.
b He had a real American breakfast.
c Paula understands the Americans better than Philip.
d She is working hard at the conference.
e There are shops in the hotel with skateboards.

6

a Sheila played badminton every weekend.
b I will do a lot of driving in my new job.
c Philip and Paula have arrived in New York.
d Mr Jones was a teacher at our school.
e Kevin is drinking some coffee.
f I've been at the cinema.
g We are going to have fish and chips on Friday.
h Joe is unpacking his suitcase.

7

a Has she been to America before?
b Has Paula gone to the airport?
c Have you reserved a rental car in New York?
d Have you had any tea, yet?
e Has she repaired the hairdryer for you?
f Have you picked up the boss from the airport?
g Have they played tennis before?

8

Mögliche Antworten:
I've ... had some coffee / phoned a friend / packed my suitcase / missed the bus / listened to some music / checked my e-mails / done some shopping / been happy;
I haven't ... had any coffee / phoned a friend / packed my suitcase / missed the bus / listened to any music / checked my e-mails / done any shopping / been happy

9
Individuelle Antworten:
Yes, I have./No, I haven't

16
EIN NOTFALL

Fragen zum Dialog
Teil 1: right — A young man
Teil 2: an ambulance. —
very slowly

1
Lösungsmöglichkeiten z. B.:
a eyes, ears, lips, shoulders,
arms, hands, wrists, legs, feet
b head, face, nose, mouth, back

2
a eyes
b teeth
c fingers
d shoulders
e hair
f toes
g faces
h nose

3
a left
b to hit
c slow
d to break
e painful
f to knock down
g to fall
h ambulance
i pavement
j necessary

4
a Suddenly
b Luckily
c carefully
d honestly
e quickly
f slowly

5
a I was checking my e-mails
in the office yesterday
morning.
b She was planning her trip to
America yesterday afternoon.
c They were playing bad-
minton at the sports
centre yesterday evening.
d He was tidying his room at
home this morning.
e I was doing some shopping
in/at Chapel Market this
afternoon.

6
1 wrist hurts / not broken —
don't use it for the next
week / cream
2 toe hurts / not broken —
take it easy / don't go for
any walks
3 tooth painful — injection /
not eat or drink anything for
the next hours

7
a were walking, started
b was cooking, arrived
c saw, were you waiting
d was watching, called
e was unpacking, had
f was leaving, met

8
a She was shopping in Islington
with a friend.
b She was knocked down from
behind by a young skate-
boarder.
c Yes, it was (broken).
d No, luckily there was a
doctor there.
e Her wrist was very
painful.
f He called an ambulance.
g The police have talked to
the young man.
h Skateboarding on the
pavement is a real problem.

17
AUF DEM POLIZEIREVIER

Fragen zum Dialog
Teil 1: her wallet. — right
Teil 2: black leather
— ten o'clock.

1
a blue
b green
c yellow
d red
e blond(e)
f dark
g black and white
h grey

2
CNDHDI**YELLOW**DEIWRDKFODNEN
DUUZ**BLUE**DBRYOKEUDKKINUUER
W**RED**DKWIUZZABOTDKDIESUZTTZ
GREENYXFS**GREY**SLIGJIKOIP**BLACK**
UGJURHZZR**WHITE**DKIZTUHDDEZZ
HBDTBVVTYFRJHJNZ**ORANGE**FKMV
NHFTR**BROWN**PLGOTHIUZTGEDJDJ
EJBBDE**PURPLE**DHDEJJENDUFHZH
TTDKNNFJUZDEZZTFHKWRDCSVE

3
a telephone
b leather
c family
d elderly
e bench
f money
g to steal
h to end
i to lose
j mine

4
Lösungsvorschlag:
Sheila bedankt sich dafür, dass
Colin West ihre Brieftasche
abgegeben hat. Sie hat den
gemeinsamen Kaffee genossen
und würde sich freuen, mal
wieder zusammen einen Kaffee
zu trinken. Sie berichtet, dass
ihr Sohn und ihr Enkel viel
unterwegs sind. Und da ihr
Mann bereits gestorben ist,
fühlt sie sich oft einsam.

5
a My, yours
b her
c your, ours
d Theirs, Yours
e yours
f mine
g my, theirs

6
a Someone has stolen Mrs
Cook's bag.
b It has never happened to
her before.
c Her bag is brown leather
with a credit card and about
£7 in it.
d Mrs Cook was sitting on a
park bench.
e The money is gone.
f The police officer has to write
a report first.

7
a went
b has stolen
c has never
happened
d went
e took
f left
g I've just
found

8

1 f	4 e	7 b
2 g	5 c	
3 a	6 d	

9

a Philip has already done some work.
b I saw my mother yesterday.
c Jenny arrived at the station at ten o'clock.
d We went to the theatre last Friday.
e They have not yet found the wallet.
f I took my son to see the doctor on Thursday.

18

EIN AUSFLUG

Fragen zum Dialog
Teil 1: at Manchester University. — in the 13th century.
Teil 2: doesn't like — wrong

1

a 4	c 1	e 2
b 3	d 5	

2

Waagerecht: suit, tie, shoes, tights, blouse, shirt, dress, cardigan, jumper
Senkrecht: skirt, trousers, scarf

3

a river	f to look up
b beautiful	g pole
c to park	h long
d town	i to push
e to use	j to explore

4

Where?
Oxford, Paddington Station, market, bookshops, river
When?
this Saturday, morning, leave nine o'clock, arrive eleven o'clock
What?
by train, walk round centre of town, go shopping, colleges, on a punt

5

a Exploring
b walking
c playing
d skateboarding
e tidying
f visiting
g cooking

6

a to see/visit/explore
b to go
c to see
d to walk
e learn/see
f seeing/visiting/exploring
g going
h punting
i seeing
j visiting

7

a isn't it?
b is it?
c do you?
d did you?
e isn't there?
f aren't there?

8

a punting	e have got
b invited	f am living
c asked	g get away from
d to move	h will stay

AT

ABSCHLUSSTEST

1

a Will the trip be in September?
b Will/Won't the hotel be very expensive?
c Will the conference last two days?
d Will/Won't they have time for everything?
e Will the information be ready in an hour?
f Will you have a coffee after that?

2

a awfully	d slowly.
b terribly	e fantastically
c fast	f well.

3

a must	d should
b mustn't	e would
c needn't	f have to

4

a isn't it?
b isn't there?
c is it?
d can she?
e wouldn't it?
f wasn't it?

5

a Pick up your rental car.
b Your voucher and your driver's license.
c The shuttle runs from AirTrain Station C.
d On the Van Wyck Expressway.
e Your car keys (and your car).
f All the cars have a navigation system.

6

a Exploring	d to go
b seeing	e to take
c visiting	f look up

7

a Couldn't we do that now?
b We only have to change once.
c We have to check in over there.
d Where do we go?
e We'd like to pick up a rental car.
f I've never stayed at a hotel like this before.
g I'm looking forward to a real American breakfast.
h I'll/I'm going to make a cup of tea with lots of sugar.

8

1 New York City; the Empire State Building or Central Park
2 London; St Paul's Cathedral or the Globe Theatre
3 Cambridge; King's College Chapel or the market

UNREGELMÄSSIGE VERBEN

einfache Verg.   *Stellenwort des Verg*

GRUND-FORM		SIMPLE PAST	PARTIZIP PERFEKT
be	sein	was/were	been
begin	beginnen	began	begun
break	(zer)brechen	broke	broken
buy	kaufen	bought	bought
catch	fangen; erreichen	caught	caught
come	kommen	came	come
do	tun, machen	did	done
drink	trinken	drank	drunk
drive	fahren	drove	driven
eat	essen	ate	eaten
fall	fallen	fell	fallen
feel	fühlen	felt	felt
find	finden	found	found
fly	fliegen	flew	flown
forget	vergessen	forgot	forgotten
get	bekommen	got	got
give	geben	gave	given
go	gehen	went	gone
have	haben	had	had
hear	hören	heard	heard
hurt	weh tun	hurt	hurt
keep	behalten; weiter (tun)	kept	kept
leave	verlassen	left	left
let	lassen	let	let
lie	liegen	lay	lain
lose	verlieren	lost	lost
make	machen	made	made

GRUND-FORM		SIMPLE PAST	PARTIZIP PERFEKT
mean	bedeuten	meant	meant
meet	treffen	met	met
pay	(be)zahlen	paid	paid
put	setzen, stellen, legen	put	put
read	lesen	read	read
ring	klingeln	rang	rung
run	laufen	ran	run
say	sagen	said	said
see	sehen	saw	seen
sell	verkaufen	sold	sold
send	senden	sent	sent
show	zeigen	showed	shown
sit	sitzen	sat	sat
sleep	schlafen	slept	slept
speak	sprechen	spoke	spoken
spend	verbringen; ausgeben	spent	spent
steal	stehlen	stole	stolen
stick	feststecken	stuck	stuck
take	nehmen; bringen	took	taken
tell	erzählen	told	told
think	denken	thought	thought
under-stand	verstehen	under-stood	under-stood
wear	(Kleidung) tragen	wore	worn
write	schreiben	wrote	written

287

GRAMMATISCHE BEGRIFFE

IM BUCH VERWENDETER BEGRIFF	ANDERE BEZEICHNUNG	BEISPIEL
Adjektiv	Eigenschaftswort, *adjective*	a **big** car
Adverb	Umstandswort, *adverb*	**slowly, now, here**
Bedingungssatz	Konditionalsatz, *conditional sentence, if-clause*	She will **if she can.**
Befehlsform	Imperativ, *imperative*	**Call** me any time.
bestimmter Artikel	bestimmtes Geschlechtswort, *definite article*	**the** car, **the** woman
Demonstrativpronomen	hinweisendes Fürwort, *demonstrative pronoun*	**this** car
Diphthong	Doppellaut, *diphthong*	**au, ei, eu**
direktes Objekt	direkte Satzergänzung, *direct object*	I can hear **you.**
Frageanhängsel	*question tag*	It's great, **isn't it?**
Fragewort	Interrogativpronomen, *interrogative pronoun*	**What?, How?**
Gegenwart	Präsens, *present tense*	I usually **arrive** at six.
Gerund	von einem Verb abgeleitetes Substantiv, *gerund*	I like **swimming.**
Grundform (des Verbs)	Infinitiv, *infinitive*	**(to) go**
Grundzahl	Kardinalzahl, *cardinal number*	**one, two, three**
Hilfsverb	Hilfszeitwort, *auxiliary verb*	**can, must, have**
indirektes Objekt	indirekte Satzergänzung, *indirect object*	You can go with **him.**
Komparativ	1. Steigerungsstufe des Adjektivs, *comparative*	**better, more expensive**
Konjunktion	Bindewort, *conjunction*	**and, but**
Konsonant	Mitlaut, *consonant*	**b, c, d, f**
Mengenangaben (bestimmte/unbestimmte)	Indefinitpronomen, unbestimmtes Fürwort, *indefinite pronoun*	**some, any**
modales Hilfsverb	Tätigkeitswort der Art und Weise	**can, must**
Objekt	Satzergänzung, *object*	Hazel drives **the car.**

IM BUCH VERWENDETER BEGRIFF	ANDERE BEZEICHNUNG	BEISPIEL
Ordnungszahl	Ordinalzahl, *ordinal number*	**first, second, third**
Partizip Perfekt	Mittelwort der Vergangenheit, *past participle*	**worked, been**
Passiv	Leideform, *passive voice*	It **was built.**
past progressive	Verlaufsform der Vergangenheit	He **was walking.**
Personalpronomen	persönliches Fürwort, *personal pronoun*	**I, you, he**
Plural	Mehrzahl, *plural*	three **cars**
Possessivpronomen	besitzanzeigendes Fürwort, *possessive pronoun*	**my** friend The book is **mine.**
Präposition	Verhältniswort, *preposition*	**by, for, in**
present perfect	vollendete Gegenwart, Perfekt	He **has worked** hard.
present progressive	Verlaufsform der Gegenwart	They **are watching** TV.
Reflexivpronomen	rückbezügliches Fürwort, *reflexive pronoun*	hurt **yourself,** enjoy **oneself**
Relativpronomen	bezügliches Fürwort, *relative pronoun*	**who, which, that**
Relativsatz	bezüglicher Nebensatz, *relative clause*	the woman **who is sitting at the counter**
simple past	einfache Vergangenheit, Präteritum	She **went** to school.
simple present	einfache Gegenwart, Präsens	I **like** the parade.
Singular	Einzahl, *singular*	one **car**
Subjekt	Satzgegenstand, *subject*	I saw the man.
Substantiv	Hauptwort, Nomen, *noun*	**car, house**
Superlativ	2. Steigerungsstufe des Adjektivs, *superlative*	**best, most expensive**
unbestimmter Artikel	unbestimmtes Geschlechtswort, *indefinite article*	**a** bagel, **an** egg
Verb	Zeitwort, Tätigkeitswort, *verb*	**to go, to come, to buy**
Verlaufsform	-ing Form des Verbs, *progressive form*	I'm **reading** a book.
Vokal	Selbstlaut, *vowel*	**a, e, i, o, u**
Zukunft	Futur, *future tense*	I'll **open** the window. It's **going to** rain.

AUSSPRACHE

Die Aussprache der Wörter wird im Wörterverzeichnis ab Seite 292 in eckigen Klammern in Lautschrift angegeben. Folgende Zeichen werden verwendet:

Konsonanten

ZEICHEN	BEISPIEL	PHONETIK	AUSSPRACHE
[p]	point, pot	[pɔɪnt], [pɒt]	**P**unkt
[b]	begin, hobby	[bɪ'gɪn], ['hɒbɪ]	**B**erg
[f]	feel, wife	[fiːl], [waɪf]	**F**uß
[v]	van, live	[væn], [lɪv]	**V**illa
[w]	word, forward	[wɜːd], ['fɔːwəd]	keine dt. Entsprechung, gesprochen wie **u** mit gestülpten Lippen
[t]	talk, butter	[tɔːk], ['bʌtə]	**T**on
[d]	do, red	[duː], [red]	**D**ach
[s]	save, fast	[seɪv], [fɑːst]	Schlu**ss**
[z]	zero, news	['zɪərəʊ], [njuːz]	**S**onne
[θ]	thank, breath	[θæŋk], [breθ]	keine dt. Entsprechung, gesprochen wie ein gelispeltes stimmloses **s**
[ð]	the, breathe	[ðə], [briːð]	keine dt. Entsprechung, gesprochen wie ein gelispeltes stimmhaftes **s**
[ʃ]	shop, dish	[ʃɒp], [dɪʃ]	**Sch**ule
[ʒ]	vision, garage	['vɪʒn], ['gærɑːʒ]	Passa**g**ier
[tʃ]	child, match	[tʃaɪld], [mætʃ]	deu**tsch**
[dʒ]	jeans, fudge	[dʒiːnz], [fʌdʒ]	**Dsch**ungel
[l]	land, ball	[lænd], [bɔːl]	**L**iebe
[g]	give, dog	[gɪv], [dɒg]	**g**eben
[k]	car, lake	[kɑː], [leɪk]	**k**önnen
[m]	man, room	[mæn], [ruːm]	**M**ann
[n]	note, run	[nəʊt], [rʌn]	**N**ote
[ŋ]	king, singer	[kɪŋ], ['sɪŋə]	Kli**ng**el
[r]	ring, lorry	[rɪŋ], ['lɒrɪ]	keine dt. Entsprechung, **r** gesprochen mit zurückgezogener Zunge
[h]	hotel, downhill	[həʊ'tel], [daʊn'hɪl]	**H**otel
[j]	year, beyond	[jɪə], [bɪ'jɒnd]	**j**etzt

Vokale und Diphthonge

ZEICHEN	BEISPIEL	PHONETIK	AUSSPRACHE
[æ]	hat, bad	[hæt], [bæd]	keine dt. Entsprechung, zwischen **a** und **ä**
[ʌ]	sun, other	[sʌn], [ˈʌðə]	kl**a**tschen
[e]	letter, end	[ˈletə], [end]	n**e**tt
[ə]	address, sister	[əˈdres], [ˈsɪstə]	bitt**e**
[ɪ]	visit, busy	[ˈvɪzɪt], [ˈbɪzi]	H**i**lfe
[ɒ]	clock, shop	[klɒk], [ʃɒp]	D**o**tter
[ʊ]	book, push	[bʊk], [pʊʃ]	M**u**tter
[ɑ:]	father, arm	[ˈfɑ:ðə], [ɑ:m]	K**a**hn
[i:]	teach, fifteen	[ti:tʃ], [ˌfɪfˈti:n]	B**ie**ne
[ɔ:]	call, altogether	[kɔ:l], [ˌɔ:ltəˈgeðə(r)]	Z**o**rn
[ɜ:]	bird, world, earn	[bɜ:d], [wɜ:ld], [ɜ:n]	f**ö**rdern
[u:]	news, boom	[nju:z], [bu:m]	St**u**hl
[aɪ]	find, idea	[faɪnd], [aɪˈdɪə]	M**ei**ster
[eɪ]	place, able	[pleɪs], [eɪbl]	keine dt. Entsprechung, Lautfolge von [e] + [ɪ]
[ɔɪ]	voice, enjoy	[vɔɪs], [ɪnˈdʒɔɪ]	l**äu**ten
[aʊ]	town, out	[taʊn], [aʊt]	H**au**s
[əʊ]	road, open	[rəʊd], [ˈəʊpən]	keine dt. Entsprechung, Lautfolge von [ə] + [ʊ]
[eə]	bear, air, where	[beə], [eə], [weə]	popul**ä**r
[ɪə]	year, ear, here	[jɪə], [ɪə], [hɪə]	v**ie**r
[ʊə]	Europe, tourism	[ˈjʊərəp], [ˈtʊərɪzm]	keine dt. Entsprechung, Lautfolge von [ʊ] + [ə]

Betonung

Im Englischen wird meist die erste Silbe des Worts betont. Bei mehrsilbigen Wörtern zeigt das Betonungszeichen [ˈ] an, dass die folgende Silbe am stärksten betont wird. Eine Nebenbetonung in einem Wort wird durch das Zeichen [ˌ] gekennzeichnet.

Das Symbol [:] bedeutet, dass der voranstehende Vokal lang gesprochen wird.

Schreibweise

In der Regel werden englische Wörter kleingeschrieben. Jedoch werden alle Eigennamen, das Personalpronomen I, die Wochentage, die Monatsnamen, sich auf Länder beziehende Adjektive (*English, German*) sowie der Satzanfang großgeschrieben.

Wörter-verzeichnis

banana 249
[bəˈnɑːnə]
Banane

bankcard 247
[ˈbæŋˌkɑːd]
Bankkarte

bar 54
[bɑː]
Theke; Bar

bathtub 220
[ˈbæθtʌb]
Badewanne

to be afraid 93
[tə biː əˈfreɪd]
Angst haben

to be born 159
[tə biː ˈbɔːn]
geboren werden

to be fond of 266
[tə biː fɒnd əv]
sehr gern
haben

to be gone 247
[tə biː ˈgɒn]
weg sein, ver-
schwunden sein

to be good at 114
[tə biː ˈgʊd æt]
gut sein in

to be interested
in 261
[tə biː ˈɪntrəstɪd ɪn]
interessiert
sein an

to be keen on 266
[tə biː ˈkiːn ɒn]
sehr mögen

to be lucky 233
[tə biː ˈlʌki]
Glück haben

to be sorry 230
[tə biː ˈsɒri]
leidtun

to be used to 205
[tə biː ˈjuːst tə]
gewöhnt sein
an

beach 208
[biːtʃ]
Strand

beautiful 258
[ˈbjuːtəfl]
schön

because 159
[bɪˈkɒz]
weil

to become 59
[tə bɪˈkʌm]
werden

bed 220
[bed]
Bett

beef 156
[biːf]
Rindfleisch

been 216
[biːn]
gewesen

beer 57
[bɪə(r)]
Bier

before 29, 104
[bɪˈfɔː(r)]
vor

to begin 219
[tə bɪˈgɪn]
beginnen

behind 103, 104
[bɪˈhaɪnd]
hinter, hinten

bench 247
[bentʃ]
(Park)Bank

best 60, 117
[best]
beste(r, s),
am besten

best-before date 75
[best bɪˈfɔː(r) deɪt]
Haltbarkeitsdatum

better 100
[ˈbetə(r)]
besser

bicycle 136
[ˈbaɪsɪkl]
Fahrrad

big 131
[bɪg]
groß

bill 89
[bɪl]
Rechnung

Bingo 114
[ˈbɪŋgəʊ]
Bingo

biscuit 244
[ˈbɪskɪt]
Keks

black 247, 248
[blæk]
schwarz

blond(e) 248
[blɒnd]
blond

blouse 262
[blaʊz]
Bluse

to blow 33
[bləʊ]
wehen, blasen

blue 248
[bluː]
blau

boat 100
[bəʊt]
Schiff, Boot

body 234
[ˈbɒdi]
Körper

bomb alarm 188
[bɒm əˈlɑːm]
Bombenalarm

boring 30
[ˈbɔːrɪŋ]
langweilig

boss 30
[bɒs]
Chef(in)

both 177
[bəʊθ]
beide

bottle 89
[ˈbɒtl]
Flasche

brave 59
[breɪv]
tapfer

bread 89
[bred]
Brot

to break 233
[tə ˈbreɪk]
brechen

breakfast 142
[ˈbrekfəst]
Frühstück

British 160
[ˈbrɪtɪʃ]
britisch

brother 44
[ˈbrʌðə]
Bruder

brown 248
[braʊn]
braun

bus 191
[bʌs]
Bus

bus stop 120
[ˈbʌs stɒp]
Bushaltestelle

business 174
[ˈbɪznɪs]
Geschäft, Business

business trip 174
[ˈbɪznɪs trɪp]
Geschäftsreise

but 12
[bʌt]
aber

button 194
[ˈbʌtn]
Knopf

to buy 72
[tə ˈbaɪ]
kaufen

by 86, 104, 174, 258
[baɪ]
an, bei, neben; spä-
testens bis; mit (bei
Verkehrsmitteln)

bye bye 16
[baɪ baɪ]
tschüs

C

cake 108
[keɪk]
Kuchen

call 191
[kɔːl]
(An)Ruf, Aufruf

to call 15
[tə ˈkɔːl]
rufen, anrufen,
nennen

can 12, 106
[kæn]
können

candlelit 128
[ˈkændlɪt]
Kerzenlicht-

can't stand 265
[ˌkɑːnt ˈstænd]
nicht ausstehen
können

canteen 30
[kænˈtiːn]
Kantine, Cafeteria

car 202
[kɑː(r)]
Auto

car rental 202
[kɑːˈrentl]
Autovermietung

cardigan 262
[ˈkɑːdɪgən]
Strickjacke

careful 233
[ˈkeəfəl]
vorsichtig

castle 61
[ˈkɑːsl]
Schloss, Burg

to catch 191
[tə ˈkætʃ]
fangen; erreichen

cathedral 103
[kəˈθiːdrəl]
Dom, Kathedrale

centre 177
[ˈsentə]
Zentrum

century 258
[ˈsentʃəri]
Jahrhundert

chair 220
[tʃeə]
Stuhl

to change 188
[tə ˈtʃeɪndʒ]
wechseln,
umsteigen

chapel 261
[ˈtʃæpl]
Kapelle

to chat 40
[tə ˈtʃæt]
chatten, plaudern

cheap 159
[tʃiːp]
billig

to check 30
[tə 'tʃek]
überprüfen, kontrollieren

to check in 191
[tə ˌtʃek 'ın]
einchecken

check-in desk 191
[tʃek 'ın desk]
Check-in-Schalter

Cheers! 57
[tʃıəz]
Prost!, Zum Wohl!

chef 57
[ʃef]
(Chef)Koch

child 60
[tʃaıld]
Kind

chore 142
[tʃɔː(r)]
Hausarbeit

Christmas Eve 132
[ˌkrısməs 'iːv]
Weihnachtsabend

church 209
[tʃɜːtʃ]
Kirche

cinema 131
['sınəmə]
Kino

city 159
['sıtı]
Stadt

clear 202
[klıə]
klar, verständlich

clerk 191
[klɑːk]
Angestellte(r)

close 177
[kləʊs]
nahe

to close 57
[tə 'kləʊs]
schließen

clothes 221
[kləʊðz]
Kleider

club 114
[klʌb]
Klub, Verein

coat 262
[kəʊt]
Mantel

coffee 26
['kɒfı]
Kaffee

colleague 30
['koliːg]
Kollege, Kollegin

college 258
['kɒlıdʒ]
College, Akademie

to come 15
[tə 'kʌm]
kommen

to come off 174
[tə ˌkʌm 'ɒf]
gelingen, klappen, zustande kommen

come on 72
[kʌm 'ɒn]
kommen Sie, na los

coming 43
['kʌmıŋ]
(ich) komme (schon)

company 205
['kʌmpənı]
Firma

to complain 180
[tə kəm'pleın]
sich beschweren

concert 142
['kɒnsət]
Konzert

conference 174
['kɒnfrəns]
Konferenz

to confirm 177
[tə kən'fɜːm]
bestätigen

cook 57
[kʊk]
Koch

to cook 156
[tə 'kʊk]
kochen

cooking 43
['kʊkıŋ]
Essen, Kochen

corner 89
['kɔːnə(r)]
Ecke

could 75
[kʊd]
könnte(n)

counter 202
['kaʊntə]
Schalter, Theke

country 159
['kʌntrı]
Land

cousin 44
['kʌzn]
Cousin, Cousine

crazy 128
[kreızı]
verrückt

crazy about 266
['kreızı ə'baʊt]
verrückt nach

credit card 247
['kredıt kɑːd]
Kreditkarte

cricket 118
['krıkıt]
Kricket

crisps 63
[krısps]
Chips

to cross 107
[tə 'krɒs]
überqueren, kreuzen

crossroads 206
['krɒsrəʊdz]
Kreuzung

Crown Jewels 103
[kraʊn 'dʒuːəlz]
Kronjuwelen

cup 148
[kʌp]
Tasse

D _____

Dad 40
[dæd]
Papa

to dance 118
[tə 'dɑːns]
tanzen

dangerous 117
['deındʒərəs]
gefährlich

dark-haired 248
[ˌdɑːk'heəd]
dunkelhaarig

date 75
[deıt]
Datum

daughter 44
['dɔːtə]
Tochter

day 26
[deı]
Tag

dead 40
[ded]
tot

December 76
[dı'sembə(r)]
Dezember

to decide 103
[tə dı'saıd]
entscheiden

deck 100
[dek]
(Schiffs)Deck

depressed 43, 48
[dı'prest]
bedrückt, deprimiert

to describe 244
[tə dı'skraıb]
beschreiben

desk 220
[desk]
Schreibtisch

to die 253
[tə 'daı]
sterben

different 54
['dıfrənt]
anders

difficult 57
['dıfıklt]
schwierig, schwer

dinner 128
['dınə]
Abendessen

to dislike 265
[tə dis'laik]
nicht mögen

to dive 118
[tə 'daıv]
tauchen

divorced 44
[dı'vɔːst]
geschieden

to do 29
[tə 'duː]
tun, machen

to do the dishes 180
[tə ˌduː ðə 'dıʃız]
abspülen, den Abwasch machen

doctor 230
['dɒktə]
Doktor, Arzt, Ärztin

don't (know) 12
[dəʊnt ('nəʊ)]
nicht (wissen)

don't mind 265
[dəʊnt 'maınd]
nichts dagegen haben

don't you? 117
['dəʊnt juː]
nicht wahr?

down 202
[daʊn]
hinunter, (nach) unten

downstairs 128
[ˌdaʊn'steəz]
unten (im Haus)

dress 262
[dres]
Kleid

drink 54
[drıŋk]
Getränk

to drink 26
[tə 'drıŋk]
trinken

to drive 205
[tə 'draıv]
fahren

driver 191
['draıvə]
Fahrer(in)

driver's license 205
['draɪvərs ,laɪsns]
Führerschein

E

e-mail 30
['i:meɪl]
E-Mail

each time 54
[i:tʃ 'taɪm]
jedes Mal

ear 234
[ɪə]
Ohr

to earn 179
[tʊ 'ɜ:n]
verdienen

east 160
[i:st]
Osten

Easter 132
['i:stə]
Ostern

to eat 131
[tʊ 'i:t]
essen

egg 219
[eg]
Ei

egg sunny side up 219
[eg ,sʌnɪ saɪd 'ʌp]
Spiegelei

eight 31
[eɪt]
acht

eighteen 31
[,eɪ'ti:n]
achtzehn

eighteenth 58
[,eɪ'ti:nθ]
achtzehnte(r, s)

eighth 58
[eɪtθ]
achte(r, s)

eighty 31
['eɪtɪ]
achtzig

elderly 247
['eldəlɪ]
ältere(r, s)

eleven 31
[ɪ'levn]
elf

eleventh 58
[ɪ'levnθ]
elfte(r, s)

else 89
[els]
sonst

end 128
[end]
Ende

to end 244
[tə 'end]
enden; beenden

to enjoy 89, 128
[tʊ ɪn'dʒɔɪ]
genießen

Enjoy your meal! 89
[ɪn,dʒɔɪ jə 'mi:l]
Guten Appetit!

to escape 251
[ɪs'keɪp]
entkommen, entwischen

even 114
['i:vn]
sogar

evening 43
['i:vnɪŋ]
Abend

ever 251
['evə]
jemals

every 29
['evrɪ]
jede(r, s)

everything 12
['evrɪθɪŋ]
alles

excellent 103
['eksələnt]
hervorragend

excuse me 202
[ɪk'skju:z mi]
Entschuldigung

exit 213
['eksɪt]
Ausgang, Ausfahrt

expensive 43
[ɪk'spensɪv]
teuer

expert 15
['ekspɜ:t]
Experte, Expertin

to explore 258
[tʊ ɪk'splɔ:(r)]
erkunden, auskundschaften

eye 234
[aɪ]
Auge

F

fabric 59
['fæbrɪk]
Stoff

face 234
[feɪs]
Gesicht

factory 59
['fæktrɪ]
Fabrik

to fall 233
[tə 'fɔ:l]
fallen

family 247
['fæmlɪ]
Familie

famous 103, 266
['feɪməs]
berühmt

fantastic 103
[fæn'tæstɪk]
fantastisch

fast 191
[fɑ:st]
schnell

father 44
['fɑ:ðə]
Vater

February 76
['febrʊərɪ]
Februar

to feel 40
[tə 'fi:l]
(sich) fühlen

feet 234
[fi:t]
Füße

fifteen 31
[,fɪf'ti:n]
fünfzehn

fifteenth 58
[,fɪf'ti:nθ]
fünfzehnte(r, s)

fifth 58
[fɪfθ]
fünfte(r, s)

fifty 31
['fɪftɪ]
fünfzig

fifty-fifty 89
[fɪftɪ'fɪftɪ]
halbe-halbe

film 142
[fɪlm]
Film

to find 43
[tə 'faɪnd]
finden

to find out 219
[tə faɪnd 'aʊt]
herausfinden

fine 12
[faɪn]
fein, prima

finger 234
['fɪŋgə]
Finger

to finish 265
[tə 'fɪnɪʃ]
beenden

first 29, 58
[fɜ:st]
zuerst, erste(r, s)

to fish 94, 118
[tə 'fɪʃ]
angeln

five 31
[faɪv]
fünf

flat 43
[flæt]
Wohnung

flight 177
[flaɪt]
Flug

floor 219
[flɔ:]
Fußboden, Etage

flower 131
['flaʊə]
Blume

to fly 136
[tə 'flaɪ]
fliegen

food 156
[fu:d]
Essen

foot 234
[fʊt]
Fuß

for 26, 104
[fɔ:]
für

foreign 43
['fɒrən]
ausländisch

to forget 131
[tə 'fə'get]
vergessen

forty 31
['fɔ:tɪ]
vierzig

founded 258
['faʊndɪd]
gegründet

four 31
[fɔ:]
vier

fourteen 31
[,fɔ:'ti:n]
vierzehn

fourteenth 58
[,fɔ:'ti:nθ]
vierzehnte(r, s)

fourth 58
[fɔ:θ]
vierte(r, s)

foyer 216
['fɔɪeɪ]
Eingangshalle, Foyer

France 160
[frɑ:ns]
Frankreich

free 174
[fri:]
frei

French 160
[frentʃ]
französisch

fresh 72
[freʃ]
frisch

Friday 132
['fraɪdeɪ]
Freitag

fridge 220
[frɪdʒ]
Kühlschrank

friend 40
[frend]
Freund(in)

from 12, 104
[frɒm]
aus, von

fruit 72
[fruːt]
Obst

fun 100
[fʌn]
Spaß

future 233
['fjuːtʃə]
Zukunft

G _____

garden 159
['gɑːdn]
Garten

German 57, 160
['dʒɜːmən]
deutsch

Germany 160
['dʒɜːmənɪ]
Deutschland

to get 54, 59
[tə 'get]
bekommen, holen

to get (to) 188
[tə 'get (,tə)]
hinkommen, ankommen

to get home 29
[tə ,get 'həʊm]
nach Hause kommen

to get off 103
[tə ,get 'ɒf]
aussteigen

ghost 61
[gəʊst]
Geist, Gespenst

gift 59
[gɪft]
Geschenk

girlfriend 131
['gɜːlfrend]
Freundin

to give 174
[tə 'gɪv]
geben

to go 15
[tə 'gəʊ]
gehen, fahren

to go for a walk 114
[tə ,gəʊ fər ə 'wɔːk]
einen Spaziergang machen

to go on 194, 258
[tə ,gəʊ 'ɒn]
weitermachen; teilnehmen; angehen

to go out 40
[tə ,gəʊ 'aʊt]
ausgehen, weggehen

go-ahead 174
[gəʊ ə'hed]
Zustimmung, grünes Licht

good 12
[gʊd]
gut

Good afternoon! 16
[gʊd ,ɑːftə'nuːn]
Guten Tag!

good at 114, 266
['gʊd æt]
gut in

Good evening! 16
[,gʊd 'iːvnɪŋ]
Guten Abend!

Good morning 16
[,gʊd 'mɔːnɪŋ]
Guten Morgen

Goodbye! 16
[,gʊd'baɪ]
Auf Wiedersehen

gran 145
[græn]
Oma

grandfather 44
['grænd,fɑːðə(r)]
Großvater

grandmother 44
['græn,mʌðə(r)]
Großmutter

grape 78
[greɪp]
Traube

great 43
[greɪt]
großartig

Great Britain 160
[,greɪt 'brɪtn]
Großbritannien

green 248
[griːn]
grün

grey 248
[greɪ]
grau

grocer 72
['grəʊsə(r)]
Lebensmittel-händler(in)

group 33
[gruːp]
Gruppe

guided tour 258
[,gaɪdɪd 'tʊə]
Führung

H _____

hairdryer 220
['heədraɪə]
Föhn

half 72
[hɑːf]
Hälfte, halb

hand 233
[hænd]
Hand

to happen 244
[tə 'hæpən]
geschehen, passieren

happy 40
['hæpɪ]
glücklich

hard 128
[hɑːd]
hart, schwer

hardly ever 40
['hɑːdlɪ ,evə(r)]
fast nie

hash browns 219
[,hæʃ 'braʊnz]
Kartoffelpuffer, Rösti

to hate 264
[tə 'heɪt]
hassen

to have (got) 12
[tə 'hæv ('gɒt)]
haben

to have a look at … 177
[tə hæv ə 'lʊk æt]
einen Blick auf … werfen

to have a word with somebody 128
[tə hæv ə 'wɜːd wɪð 'sʌmbədɪ]
mit jemandem (ein Wörtchen) reden

to have coffee 35, 180
[tə hæv 'kɒfɪ]
Kaffee trinken

to have lunch 28
[tə hæv 'lʌntʃ]
zu Mittag essen

to have to 177
[tə 'hæv tə]
müssen

haven't you? 100
['hæv(ə)nt juː]
nicht wahr?

he 17
[hiː]
er

head 15, 234
[hed]
Kopf; Leiter(in)

to hear 146
[tə 'hɪə]
hören

heavy 188
['hevɪ]
schwer, stark

Hello! 16
[hə'ləʊ]
Hallo!

to help 15
[tə 'help]
helfen

her 34, 92
[hɜː]
sie, ihr(e)

here 15
[hɪə(r)]
hier

here you are 26
['hɪə(r) juː aː(r)]
bitte schön

hers 252
[hɜːz]
ihrs

herself 120
[hə'self]
sie (selbst), sich

Hi! 16
[haɪ]
Hallo!

to hike 118
[tə 'haɪk]
wandern

him 15, 92
[hɪm]
ihn, ihm

himself 120
[hɪm'self]
er (selbst), sich

his 15, 34, 252
[hɪz]
sein(e), seins

to hit 233
[tə 'hɪt]
treffen, schlagen

holiday 132
['hɒlədeɪ]
Feiertag

home 159
[həʊm]
Zuhause

homework 117
['həʊmwɜːk]
Hausaufgaben

honest 43
['ɒnɪst]
ehrlich

to **hope** 174
[θə 'həʊp]
hoffen

hot 216
[hɒt]
heiß

hotel 177
[həʊ'tel]
Hotel

hour 29
['aʊə]
Stunde

house 142
[haʊs]
Haus

household 128
['haʊshəʊld]
Haushalt

how 75, 178
[haʊ]
wie

How about ...? 86
[haʊ ə'baʊt]
Wie wär's mit ...?

How are you? 16
[ˌhaʊ ɑː juː]
Wie geht's dir?,
Wie geht es Ihnen?

How much? 178
[haʊ 'mʌtʃ]
Wie viel?

hundred and
one 31
['hʌndrəd ænd 'wʌn]
hundertundeins,
einhundertundeins

to **hurry** 100
[tə 'hʌri]
sich beeilen

to **hurt** 117, 230
[tə 'hɜːt]
verletzen,
weh tun

husband 44
['hʌzbənd]
Ehemann

I

I 17
[aɪ]
ich

I would like 54
[aɪ wʊd 'laɪk]
ich möchte
gerne

I'd like 54
[aɪd 'laɪk]
ich möchte gerne

idea 15
[aɪ'dɪə]
Idee

if 191
[ɪf]
wenn

ill 164
[ɪl]
krank

to **imagine** 265
[ɪ'mædʒɪn]
sich vorstellen

immediately 188
[ɪ'miːdɪətlɪ]
sofort, umgehend

impression 216
[ɪm'preʃn]
Eindruck

in 12, 104
[ɪn]
in; auf

in English 57
[ɪn 'ɪŋglɪʃ]
auf Englisch

in time 191
[ɪn 'taɪm]
rechtzeitig

Indian 131
['ɪndɪən]
indisch; Inder(in)

information 177
[ɪnfə'meɪʃn]
Information(en)

inside 100
[ɪn'saɪd]
hinein, drinnen

instead of 266
[ɪn'sted ɒv]
(an)statt

interest 40
['ɪntrəst]
Interesse

interested in 266
['ɪntrəstɪd ɪn]
interessiert an

international 89
[ˌɪntə'næʃnəl]
international

into 104
['ɪntə]
in (hinein)

Ireland 160
['aɪələnd]
Irland

Irish 160
['aɪərɪʃ]
irisch

it 17, 92
[ɪt]
es; ihm

Italian 75, 160
[ɪ'tælɪən]
italienisch;
Italiener(in)

Italy 160
['ɪtəlɪ]
Italien

its 34, 252
[ɪts]
sein(e), seins

itself 120
[ɪt'self]
es (selbst),
sich

J

jacket 262
['dʒækɪt]
Jackett, Blazer

January 76
['dʒænjʊərɪ]
Januar

to **join** 181
[dʒɔɪn]
mitmachen,
sich anschließen

July 76
[dʒʊ'laɪ]
Juli

to **jump** 237
[tə 'dʒʌmp]
springen

jumper 262
['dʒʌmpə]
Pullover

June 75, 76
[dʒuːn]
Juni

just 15, 216
[dʒʌst]
einfach, nur;
gerade, eben

just a minute 54
[ˌdʒʌst ə 'mɪnɪt]
einen Augenblick

K

to **keep** 103
[tə 'kiːp]
aufbewahren,
behalten

key 205
[kiː]
Schlüssel

kilo 72
['kiːləʊ]
Kilo

to **knock (down)** 230
[tə nɒk 'daʊn]
umstoßen

to **know** 12
[tə 'nəʊ]
kennen,
wissen

L

lady 72
['leɪdɪ]
Dame

lake 119
[leɪk]
See

lamb 156
[læm]
Lamm,
Lammfleisch

landlady 43
['lændleɪdɪ]
Vermieterin

last 57, 247
['lɑːst]
letzte(r, s); zuletzt

to **last** 174
[tə 'lɑːst]
dauern

late 89, 188
[leɪt]
spät, zu spät

later 177
['leɪtə]
später

to **learn** 156
[tə 'lɜːn]
lernen,
erfahren

leather 247
['leðə]
Leder

to **leave** 54, 188
[tə 'liːv]
verlassen,
abreisen

left 230
[left]
links

leg 230, 234
[leg]
Bein

to **let** 145
[tə 'let]
lassen

let's, let
us 89
[lets, 'let ʌz]
lass(t) uns,
lassen Sie uns

life 29
[laɪf]
Leben

light 216, 220
[laɪt]
Licht

like 29
[laɪk]
wie, als

to **like** 40
[tə 'laɪk]
mögen, gern haben

like that 54
[ˌlaɪk 'ðæt]
so, auf diese Weise

to **like... better** 117
[tə ˌlaɪk ... 'betə]
... lieber mögen

lips 234
[lɪps]
Lippen

nineteen 31
[ˌnaɪnˈtiːn]
neunzehn

nineteenth 58
[ˌnaɪnˈtiːnθ]
neunzehnte(r, s)

ninety 31
[ˈnaɪntɪ]
neunzig

ninth 58
[naɪnθ]
neunte(r, s)

no 26
[nəʊ]
nein; kein(e)

no one 78
[ˈnəʊ wʌn]
niemand

north 160
[nɔːθ]
Norden

nose 131, 234
[nəʊz]
Nase

not 26
[nɒt]
nicht

not … anyone 78
[nɒt … ˈɛnɪwʌn]
niemand

not …
anything 78
[nɒt … ˈɛnɪθɪŋ]
nichts

not …
anywhere 78
[nɒt … ˈɛnɪweə]
nirgendwo

not … yet 219
[ˌnɒt … ˈjet]
noch nicht

nothing 78
[ˈnʌθɪŋ]
nichts

November 76
[nəʊˈvembə]
November

now 15
[naʊ]
nun, jetzt

nowhere 78
[ˈnəʊweə]
nirgendwo

number 244
[ˈnʌmbə]
Nummer

O

o'clock 62
[əˈklɒk]
… Uhr

October 76
[ɒkˈtəʊbə]
Oktober

of 12
[ɒv]
von

of course 75
[ɒv ˈkɔːs]
natürlich

office 12
[ˈɒfɪs]
Büro

officer 244
[ˈɒfɪsə]
(Polizei)Beamter,
(Polizei)Beamtin

often 29, 33
[ˈɒfn]
oft

old 40
[əʊld]
alt

on 40, 104
[ɒn]
an, auf, in, im

on the right 202
[ˌɒn ðə ˈraɪt]
rechts

on the way 188
[ˌɒn ðə ˈweɪ]
unterwegs

once 188
[wʌns]
einmal

once again 219
[wʌns əˈgen]
noch einmal

one 31
[wʌn]
eins

one hundred 31
[ˌwʌn ˈhʌndrəd]
hundert

one hundred and
one 31
[ˌwʌn ˈhʌndrəd ænd
ˈwʌn]
hundertundeins,
einhundertundeins

only 188
[ˈəʊnlɪ]
nur

open 100
[ˈəʊpən]
offen

or 29
[ɔː]
oder

orange 75
[ˈɒrɪndʒ]
Orange,
Apfelsine

orange 248
[ˈɒrɪndʒ]
orangefarben

our 15, 34
[ˈaʊə]
unser(e)

ours 252
[ˈaʊə(r)z]
unseres

ourselves 120
[aʊəˈselvz]
wir (selbst), uns

out 142
[aʊt]
hinaus,
draußen

outside 188
[aʊtˈsaɪd]
draußen, nach
draußen

over there 86
[eʊvə ˈðeə]
dort drüben

P

painful 233
[ˈpeɪnfʊl]
schmerzhaft

parade 48
[pəˈreɪd]
Umzug, Parade

parents 44
[ˈpeərənts]
Eltern

park 114
[pɑːk]
Park

to park 206, 258
[tə ˈpɑːk]
parken

passenger 188
[ˈpæsɪndʒə]
Passagier(in)

past 188
[pɑːst]
nach (zeitlich)

pavement 230
[ˈpeɪvmənt]
Bürgersteig

to pay 54
[tə ˈpeɪ]
bezahlen

peace 131
[piːs]
Frieden, Ruhe

pear 106
[peə]
Birne

penguin 33
[ˈpeŋgwɪn]
Pinguin

penny 75
[ˈpenɪ]
Penny (Pl pence)

people 26
[ˈpiːpl]
Leute, Menschen

performance 103
[pəˈfɔːməns]
Aufführung

perhaps 86
[pəˈhæps]
vielleicht

personally 216
[ˈpɜːsənəlɪ]
persönlich

phone 30
[fəʊn]
Telefon

to phone 40
[tə ˈfəʊn]
anrufen

photo 103
[ˈfəʊtəʊ]
Foto

photograph 59
[ˈfəʊtəgræf]
Foto

photographer 59
[fəˈtɒgrəfə]
Fotograf(in)

to pick up 202
[tə ˌpɪk ˈʌp]
abholen

pier 100
[ˈpɪə]
Landungssteg

pint 54
[paɪnt]
Pint (ca. ½ l)

place 103
[pleɪs]
Ort

to plan 30
[tə ˈplæn]
planen

plane 188
[pleɪn]
Flugzeug

to play 114
[tə ˈpleɪ]
spielen

to play football
118
[tə ˌpleɪ ˈfʊtbɔːl]
Fußball
spielen

please 26
[pliːz]
bitte

pm 62
[ˌpiːˈem]
nachmittags,
abends

poison 59
[ˈpɔɪzn]
Gift

pole 261
[pəʊl]
Stange,
Pfahl

police
station 244
[pəˈliːs ˌsteɪʃ(ə)n]
Polizeirevier

299

pork 156
[pɔːk]
Schweinefleisch

Portugal 160
['pɔːtʃəgl]
Portugal

Portuguese 160
[ˌpɔːtʃʊˈgiːz]
portugiesisch

possible 188
['pɒsəbl]
möglich

potato 156
[pəˈteɪtəʊ]
Kartoffel

pound 72
[paʊnd]
Pfund

to **pour out** 128
[tə ˌpɔːr ˈaʊt]
eingießen

to **practise** 265
[tə ˈpræktɪs]
üben

to **prefer** 114
[tə prɪˈfɜː]
vorziehen

to **press** 194
[tə ˈpres]
drücken

price 72
[praɪs]
Preis

probably 216
['prɒbəblɪ]
wahrscheinlich

problem 15
['prɒbləm]
Problem

project 30
['prɒdʒekt]
Projekt

pub 54
[pʌb]
Pub, Kneipe

punt 261
[pʌnt]
Stocherkahn

to **punt** 261
[tə ˈpʌnt]
staken

purple 248
['pɜːpl]
purpur-farben

to **push** 261
[tə ˈpʊʃ]
schieben, drücken

to **put** 128
[tə ˈpʊt]
setzen, stellen, legen

Q

question 117
['kwestʃn]
Frage

queue 100
[kjuː]
Reihe, Schlange

quickly 188
['kwɪklɪ]
schnell

quiet 128
['kwaɪət]
ruhig, leise

R

race 108
[reɪs]
(Wett)Rennen

to **rain** 33
[tə ˈreɪn]
regnen

raincoat 262
['reɪnkəʊt]
Regenmantel

rainy 164
['reɪnɪ]
regnerisch

to **read** 182
[tə ˈriːd]
lesen

ready 177
['redɪ]
fertig

real 57
[rɪəl]
echt, wirklich

to **realize** 145
[tə ˈrɪəlaɪz]
wahrnehmen, begreifen

really 43
['rɪəlɪ]
wirklich

reason 188
['riːzn]
Grund

reception 216
[rɪˈsepʃn]
Empfang, Rezeption

red 72, 248
[red]
rot

redheaded 248
['redhedɪd]
rothaarig

refrigerator 220
[rɪˈfrɪdʒəreɪtə(r)]
Kühlschrank

remote control 220
[rɪˈməʊt kənˈtrəʊl]
Fernbedienung

rental car 205
[ˌrentl ˈkɑː]
Mietwagen

to **repair** 216
[tə rɪˈpeə]
reparieren

to **repeat** 90
[tə rɪˈpiːt]
wiederholen

to **reserve** 205
[tə rɪˈzɜːv]
reservieren

restaurant 86
['restərɒnt]
Restaurant

to **ride** 118
[tə ˈraɪd]
reiten

right 43
[raɪt]
richtig

to **ring** 30
[tə ˈrɪŋ]
klingeln

river 261
['rɪvə]
Fluss

riverbank 121
['rɪvəbæŋk]
Flussufer

road 206
[rəʊd]
Straße

roast 156
[rəʊst]
Braten

roast potatoes 156
[ˌrəʊst pəˈteɪtəʊz]
Bratkartoffeln

robot 180
['rəʊbɒt]
Roboter

rock 93
[rɒk]
Felsen

room 43
[ruːm]
Zimmer, Raum

round 15, 235
[raʊnd]
rund; herum

roundabout 206
['raʊndəbaʊt]
Kreisverkehr

to **row** 94, 118
[tə ˈrəʊ]
rudern

rugby 118
['rʌgbɪ]
Rugby

to **run** 191, 202
[tə ˈrʌn]
rennen, laufen; fahren, verkehren

S

safe 205
[seɪf]
sicher

to **sail** 118
[tə ˈseɪl]
segeln

salad 86
['sæləd]
Salat

Saturday 72, 132
['sætədeɪ]
Samstag

sausage 47
['sɒsɪdʒ]
Wurst

to **say** 29
[tə ˈseɪ]
sagen

scarf 262
[skɑːf]
Schal, Halstuch

school 40
[skuːl]
Schule

Scotland 43
['skɒtlənd]
Schottland

seaside 33
['siːsaɪd]
Küste

seat 100
[siːt]
Sitz(platz)

second 58
['sekənd]
zweite(r, s)

security 188
[sɪˈkjʊərɪtɪ]
Sicherheit

to **see** 72
[tə ˈsiː]
sehen

See you soon 16
[ˌsiː juː ˈsuːn]
Bis bald

to **seem** 131
[tə ˈsiːm]
scheinen

sell-by date 75
['sel baɪ ˌdeɪt]
Verkaufsdatum

sensible 59
['sensəbl]
vernünftig

sensitive 59
['sensətɪv]
sensibel

separated 44
['sepəreɪtɪd]
getrennt

September 76
[sepˈtembə]
September

seven 31
[ˈsevn]
sieben

seventeen 31
[ˌsevnˈtiːn]
siebzehn

seventeenth 58
[ˌsevnˈtiːnθ]
siebzehnte(r, s)

seventh 58
[ˈsevnθ]
siebte(r, s)

seventy 31
[ˈsevntɪ]
siebzig

shall 177
[ʃæl]
soll(en)

shark 93
[ʃɑːk]
Hai

she 17
[ʃiː]
sie

sheep 106
[ʃiːp]
Schaf

shirt 262
[ʃɜːt]
Hemd

shoe 262
[ʃuː]
Schuh

shop 131
[ʃɒp]
Geschäft

to shop 230
[tə ˈʃɒp]
einkaufen

should 156
[ʃʊd]
sollte(n)

shoulder 234
[ˈʃəʊldə]
Schulter

to show 12
[tə ˈʃəʊ]
zeigen

shower 216
[ˈʃaʊə]
Dusche

shuttle 202
[ˈʃʌtl]
*Pendelbus,
Pendelzug*

siblings 44
[ˈsɪblɪŋz]
Geschwister

side 219
[saɪd]
Seite

sight 103
[saɪt]
Sehenswürdigkeit

sightseeing tour 114
[ˈsaɪtsiːɪŋ ˌtʊə]
Stadtrundfahrt

to sign 205
[tə ˈsaɪn]
unterschreiben

single 44
[ˈsɪŋgl]
unverheiratet, ledig

sink 220
[ˈsɪŋk]
Waschbecken

sir 86
[sɜː]
mein Herr

sister 44
[ˈsɪstə]
Schwester

to sit 86
[tə ˈsɪt]
sitzen

six 31
[sɪks]
sechs

sixteen 31
[ˌsɪksˈtiːn]
sechzehn

sixteenth 58
[ˌsɪksˈtiːnθ]
sechzehnte(r, s)

sixth 58
[sɪksθ]
sechste(r, s)

sixty 31
[ˈsɪkstɪ]
sechzig

to skate 230
[tə ˈskeɪt]
Skateboard fahren

skateboarding 117
[ˈskeɪtbɔːdɪŋ]
*Skateboard-
fahren*

to ski 118
[tə ˈskiː]
Ski fahren

skirt 262
[skɜːt]
Rock

to sleep 94
[tə ˈsliːp]
schlafen

slow 233
[sləʊ]
langsam

small 235
[smɔːl]
klein

to snore 121
[tə ˈsnɔː]
schnarchen

to snow 33
[tə ˈsnəʊ]
schneien

so 57, 177
[səʊ]
so; damit, sodass

so far 251
[səʊ ˈfɑː(r)]
bisher

soft 156
[sɒft]
weich

some 57, 78
[sʌm]
einige, etwas

someone 78, 131
[ˈsʌmwʌn]
(irgend)jemand

something 78, 156
[ˈsʌmθɪŋ]
(irgend)etwas

sometimes 29, 33
[ˈsʌmtaɪmz]
manchmal

somewhere 78
[ˈsʌmweə]
irgendwo

son 40, 44
[sʌn]
Sohn

sorry! 75
[ˈsɒrɪ]
Entschuldigung!

to sound 43
[tə ˈsaʊnd]
klingen

soup 86
[suːp]
Suppe

south 12, 160
[saʊθ]
Süden

Spain 160
[speɪn]
Spanien

Spanish 89, 160
[ˈspænɪʃ]
spanisch

to speak 89
[tə ˈspiːk]
sprechen

speciality 156
[ˌspeʃɪˈælətɪ]
Spezialität

spelling 249
[ˈspelɪŋ]
Schreibweise

to spend 142
[tə ˈspend]
*verbringen;
ausgeben*

sports 114
[spɔːts]
Sport

sports centre 142
[ˈspɔːts ˌsentə]
Sportcenter

staff 30
[stɑːf]
Personal

to stand 103
[tə ˈstænd]
stehen, sich stellen

to start 89
[tə ˈstɑːt]
beginnen, anfangen

starter 86
[ˈstɑːtə]
Vorspeise

station 188
[ˈsteɪʃn]
Station, Bahnhof

to stay 159
[tə ˈsteɪ]
bleiben

to steal 244
[tə ˈstiːl]
stehlen

still 75
[stɪl]
noch

to stop 265
[tə ˈstɒp]
aufhören

straight (on) 206
[streɪt (ˈɒn)]
(immer) geradeaus

street 72
[striːt]
Straße

strong 202
[strɒŋ]
kräftig, stark

to study 258
[tə ˈstʌdɪ]
studieren

suddenly 230
[ˈsʌdnlɪ]
plötzlich

sugar 26
[ˈʃʊgə]
Zucker

to suggest 258
[tə səˈdʒest]
vorschlagen

suit 262
[suːt]
*Anzug,
Kostüm*

suitcase 188
[ˈsuːtkeɪs]
Koffer

Sunday 100, 132
[ˈsʌndeɪ]
Sonntag

sunny 219
[ˈsʌnɪ]
sonnig

301

why 26, 178
[waɪ]
warum

widowed 44
['wɪdəʊd]
verwitwet

wife 40, 44
[waɪf]
Ehefrau

will 174
[wɪl]
*werden
(Futur)*

wind 33
[wɪnd]
Wind

window 86
['wɪndəʊ]
Fenster

wine 86
[waɪn]
Wein

with 12, 104
[wɪð]
mit, bei

without 266
[wɪð'aʊt]
ohne

woman
(Pl women) 145
['wʊmən / 'wɪmɪn]
Frau

won't 131
[wəʊnt]
nicht werden

wonderful 159
['wʌndəfl]
wundervoll

word 57
[wɜːd]
Wort

work 26, 30
[wɜːk]
Arbeit

to **work** 30, 216
[tə 'wɜːk]
*arbeiten;
funktionieren*

**working
day** 132
[,wɜːkɪŋ 'deɪ]
Werktag

would 72
[wʊd]
würde(n)

wrist 233, 234
[rɪst]
Handgelenk

to **write** 182, 223
[tə 'raɪt]
schreiben

wrong 43
[rɒŋ]
falsch

Y

year 40
[jɪə]
Jahr

yellow 248
['jeləʊ]
gelb

yes 12
[jes]
ja

yesterday
142
['jestədeɪ]
gestern

yet 216
[jet]
schon

**Yorkshire
pudding** 156
['jɔː(r)kʃə(r) ,pudɪŋ]
*Yorkshire
Pudding
(Beilage zu
Fleischgerichten)*

you 17
[juː]
du, ihr, Sie

you *(Objekt)* 92
[juː]
*dich, dir; euch;
Sie, Ihnen*

young 145
[jʌŋ]
jung

your 34
[jɔː]
*dein(e); euer(e);
Ihr(e) (Sg + Pl)*

yours 247, 252
[jɔːz]
dein(e), Ihr(e)

yourself 117
[jɔː'self]
du (selbst), dich

yourselves 120
[jɔː'selvz]
ihr (selbst), euch

Z

zero 31
['zɪərəʊ]
null

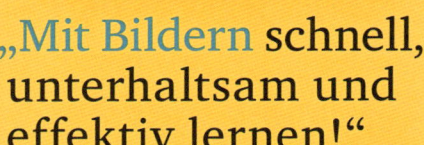